MYSTICISM

MYSTICISM
An Evangelical Option?

WINFRIED CORDUAN

ZondervanPublishingHouse
Academic and Professional Books
Grand Rapids, Michigan

A Division of HarperCollins*Publishers*

MYSTICISM: AN EVANGELICAL OPTION?
Copyright © 1991 by Winfried Corduan

Requests for information should be addressed to:
Zondervan Publishing House
Academic and Professional Books
1415 Lake Drive S.E.
Grand Rapids, Michigan 49506

Library of Congress Cataloging-in-Publication Data

Corduan, Winfried.
Mysticism : an evangelical option? / Winfried Corduan.
p.   cm.
Includes bibliographical references and index.
ISBN 0-310-52901-8
1. Mysticism—Comparative studies. 2. Evangelicalism. 3. Mysticism—
Controversial literature. 4. Mystical union. I. Title.
BL625.C67 1991   91-8326
248.2'2—dc20   CIP

Edited by Craig Noll and Leonard G. Goss
Designed by Jan M. Ortiz

Printed in the United States of America

91 92 93 94 95 96 / CH / 10 9 8 7 6 5 4 3 2 1

To Nick and Seth

Contents

Acknowledgments

I WISH TO THANK TAYLOR UNIVERSITY FOR STRONG support while writing this book. In particular I am grateful to Dean Richard Stanislaw for a budget and a sabbatical provided for my research and writing.

It was a privilege to work on this project while spending a semester at the Neues Leben Seminar in Wölmersen, West Germany. I will always remember the dialogue and fellowship with the faculty at this exciting new evangelical seminary.

I discussed preliminary conclusions in papers read at meetings of the Evangelical Theological Society, the Evangelical Philosophical Society, and the Society of Christian Philosophers. I am grateful for comments and help received, particularly for several important corrections suggested by David K. Clark of Bethel Seminary.

I thank Len Goss, academic editor at Zondervan, and his readers for making the prepublication process remarkably smooth and supportive.

Finally, I say a special "thank you!" to my wife, June, and our boys for allowing me to go off and pursue the writing of this book. I am not sure that the visits to grandparents in Linz or the sight-seeing of innumerable castles was sufficient to offset the stresses of spending most of one fall in an apartment in Germany.

1

A Personal Introduction

CUTHBERT BUTLER, A RESPECTED WRITER ON MYSTI-cism in Christendom, quotes with approval a reviewer who suggests that any author of a book on mysticism ought to begin by declaring his or her position on the subject.[1] Arthur L. Johnson divides the bibliography in his recent book into "pro-mysticism" and "anti-mysticism" literature.[2] In this way the reader knows where an author's arguments are headed and can be fortified against any unpleasant surprises. Once one knows whether an author is for or against mysticism, it is much easier to filter the ideas through one's own conceptions.

Unfortunately, marking out positions on this topic is not always easy. After all, mysticism is a phenomenon of many dimensions, as will become evident in this book. Since there are controversies connected with almost every phase of it, only an exaggerated reductionism would want to turn the whole phenomenon into one debating position: mysticism—pro or con? A look at mysticism involves presuppositions, facts, and interpretations, and one cannot always be sure where one picks up and the other leaves off. Thus it really is

---

[1]Cuthbert Butler, *Western Mysticism: The Teaching of SS Augustine, Gregory, and Bernard on Contemplation and the Contemplative Life* (New York: Dutton, 1924), v.

[2]Arthur L. Johnson, *Faith Misguided: Exposing the Dangers of Mysticism* (Chicago: Moody Press, 1988), 153–56.

not helpful to comply with the apparently simple request of raising the curtain at once and revealing to any prospective audience whether the author is presenting a work in favor or in opposition to mysticism.

The purpose of this study is to describe and evaluate the phenomenon of mysticism from an evangelical Christian point of view. The issues are complex; the questions to be raised and answered must be carefully formulated. A number of answers are acceptable only if they are very carefully qualified. Therefore it would simply not make sense to require all of the answers to be laid out in advance.

At the outset I should make a few autobiographical revelations. I have never had a classic mystical experience, one in accord with W. T. Stace's seven-point description.[3] Thus the reader can be reassured on at least one point: this book is not an *ex post facto* attempt at legitimating a prior experience of mine. Furthermore, the reader can be quite at ease that this study is not an essentially apologetic piece for the traditional mystical way of life.

But neither ought the reader to anticipate only a detached and allegedly objective work whose only purpose is to contribute to academic discussion. For even though this book concerns itself in detail with various technical issues, it is also motivated by some existential considerations. To summarize this aspect, I believe that various mystics at times say certain things that all Christians ought to be saying. Thus, in the process of examining the various dimensions of mysticism, we cannot shy away from the questions of truth and spirituality.

In some ways this book has the nature of an intellectual and spiritual quest. It was not written from the fortified citadel of having all relevant truth in hand, to be dispensed at measured intervals. The writing of this text reflects research which began a few years ago with certain presuppositions, but no detailed conclusions in mind. Thus, even though I now feel

---

[3]W. T. Stace, *Mysticism and Philosophy* (New York: St. Martin's Press, Jeremy P. Tarcher, 1960), 131–33. See chapter 2 and throughout for further discussion of these points.

quite sure about the truth of what I have discovered, it would be wrong to create the impression that I am merely recording obvious fact. A few years back some of these ideas were not at all unequivocal to me.

At the outset, it will be helpful to identify presuppositions I make in three areas: truth, theology, and methodology.

The Presupposition of Truth

I assume first that there is truth to be discovered. We might picture the study of mysticism as a quest for truth, perhaps even invoking pictures of medieval knights in pursuit of their goal. The intent of such an image would be to call attention to the struggle, the commitment, and the persistence necessary for the task. But we need to distinguish ourselves from Percival's quest for the Holy Grail, not to mention Don Quixote and other adventurers in search of what they will never find. It is not necessary to claim to have the last word on any given subject to be able to say that there is a final word to be spoken and that human beings in principle have access to it. There are answers to the questions we are asking. We can admit that we may not have all of the right answers, but that fact does not preclude the possibility that a further examination of all the evidence would reveal the correct answers.

For all their attacks on logic, speech, and objectivity, even mystics would not usually deny this presupposition. They believe that their experience is the avenue into truth. Now they may go on to say some very strange-sounding things— that their truth is superrational, that it cannot be put into words, or that it is neither objective nor subjective, but transsubjective. We shall examine all of these claims below. But there can be no denying that mystics typically think that they have discovered some truth or "ultratruth."

Thus it would not be in the spirit of mysticism to abort this project from the beginning with the claim that no final truth can be found. To cite another example (and again to foreshadow considerable discussion), mystics often say that their experience is "ineffable." There is much debate on whether it is or is not ineffable. In desperation one might want to argue that it is neither; perhaps it is "pseudoineffable" or something else yet without a name. But it must be something, and the discussion about what that property is can proceed along the line that it must be something. To say that there is no truth to be discovered would not be mystical; it would simply be muddled.

Theological Presuppositions

A second area of presupposition is theology. This inquiry is based on a thoroughly evangelical foundation. The whole point of this quest is to see what may legitimately be said within evangelical Christianity about mysticism. It can hardly be denied that outside of evangelical Christianity, mysticism holds a legitimate place in the history of human thought. One can certainly be a Hindu and be a mystic, a fact that is irrelevant for our purposes here. Our question, specifically, is whether one can be an evangelical believer and find value in mysticism. Thus, whatever in this discussion should turn out to be incompatible with evangelical Christianity needs to be ruled out of bounds in any final assessment.

Consequently, I cannot deny that my theological presuppositions are going to determine the direction of this discussion. Ninian Smart has criticized R. C. Zaehner (both very capable scholars) for allowing such an influence in his own presentation.[4] But it is clear that Smart's own interpretations are also partly determined by his personal assumptions. And, more importantly, it does not make sense to think that the attempt to approach this subject without personal theological convictions is somehow desirable. In order to come to conclusions in theological matters, one must have certain

---

[4]Ninian Smart, "Interpretation and Mystical Experience," *Religious Studies*, 1 (1965): 75–88.

theological criteria for truth. Theological convictions become detrimental only if an unreasoned theological assertion takes the place of carefully reasoned argument, theological or otherwise.

Therefore we must also distance ourselves deliberately from W. T. Stace's "principle of causal indifference." This principle states that the origin of a mystical experience is irrelevant for the evaluation of the legitimacy of the experience.[5] If one cannot isolate a decisive distinction in characteristics, then both experiences are equally eligible for labeling as true mystical experiences.

For Stace's purposes much can be said in favor of this principle. Imagine two people have a headache. Both people describe their headaches in identical ways. In that case there is no reason to say that one person has a more genuine headache than the other one, even if the first person's came from staying up all night reading philosophical classics while the second one is suffering from the effects of having had too much to drink. In the same way, if two mystics describe their experiences in identical terms, it could be a matter of indifference that one's experience was caused by a life of spiritual discipline while the other one simply took a drug for the same experience. Both experiences must be reckoned as equally legitimate.

But such words as "legitimate," "genuine," "true," and "authentic" are ambiguous when used in this context. It is beyond doubt that by common usage all experiences of certain descriptions are legitimately called mystical. But we must reject the principle of indifference if (1) these terms imply a standard by which the experience is legitimated in the sense of receiving approval or (2) these terms imply that there can be

---

[5]Stace, *Mysticism and Philosophy*, 29–32. Stace states it formally this way: "If X has an alleged mystical experience *P1* and Y has an alleged mystical experience *P2*, and if the phenomenological characteristics of *P1* entirely resemble the phenomenological characteristics of *P2* so far as can be ascertained from the descriptions given by X and Y, then the two experiences cannot be regarded as being of two different kinds . . . merely because they arise from dissimilar causal conditions" (29).

no standard beyond phenomenological description. If we are to treat the two people with headaches, knowledge of the causes will determine our evaluation and suggested remedy. Thus to scholars who have not deceived themselves into thinking that they are free of all theological inclinations, the origin of a mystical experience makes a lot of difference. The person who has taken mescaline may be truly said to have had a mystical experience, but Hindus, Christians, or Buddhists could rightly claim that such a person did not have a genuine mystical experience by their standards of authenticity. The cause of the experience does matter.

Stace can claim the principle of causal indifference because, first of all, he has tied himself to the naturalistic principle, "that all macroscopic existences and events occurring in the space-time world are explicable without exceptions by natural causes." But we cannot share this principle. Even though Stace does not intend to rule out nonmaterial reality with this principle, he does nevertheless shut the door on much traditional Christian thought. According to this principle, God (if there is such a being at all) could never interact with the world apart from natural laws. Thus for Stace miracles do not occur, and he claims that prayer as request to God to "alter the natural course of events" is nowadays so understood by "no instructed theologian."[6]

But without miracles there can be no evangelical Christianity. Certainly even some biblical events that we might call miracles are explicable with reference to natural events (e.g. the parting of the Red Sea by a strong east wind). Other events, however (e.g. turning water into wine), defy explanation on the basis of known physical laws. The same thing is true for the resurrection and for the feeding miracles. Here we do not have either the speeding up of otherwise natural processes or a fortuitous constellation of events. We cannot dismiss a priori the possibility of the miraculous from our discussion of mysticism.

---

[6]Ibid., 22–23, 24.

Similarly we must also always allow for direct divine intervention in our lives—with or without preceding prayer. To be sure, God's responses to our prayers are not always clear to us. But part of the biblical picture of prayer is that God at times grants us our requests in response to our petitions, and we could respond to Stace by saying that theologians ought to be instructed to heed this piece of information. In terms of mysticism, we cannot close the door on a person's having an experience directly due to God's action.

So far I have argued here that theological presuppositions make a difference and that we should not accommodate an antisupernatural bias in our presuppositions. From the evangelical truth presupposed here, three items deserve mention for their crucial value at the conclusion of this study.

The authority of Scripture. Evangelical Protestantism subscribes to the full authority of the Bible as understood with the doctrines of plenary inspiration and truthfulness.[7] Any theology should begin with divine revelation as contained in Scripture. It is undeniable that theologians resort to concepts from their own culture in order to express revealed truth. But the Bible must always be the standard for evaluating cultural expressions, not vice versa. The same thing is true for mysticism, the personal experience it entails, and the philosophical formulations in which it is expressed. Ultimately, a mystical experience may not be the standard for evaluating truth in the Bible, but the Bible must remain the standard by which personal realities and experiences are tested.

The theology of God. Some things are true of the biblical God that are diametrically opposed to what mystics, particularly of the Eastern varieties, contend. God is personal. He is light (1 John 1:5), not beyond light and darkness. He is the Creator, always to be distinguished from the creature. We could continue this list.

---

[7]As is well known, evangelicals are divided on the issue of how to express biblical truthfulness. Of the various options, I hold the view of biblical inerrancy: Scripture is true in all that it affirms, understood through proper exegesis.

Once again we need to beware of shortcutting all of the technical discussion involved in this topic. In a chapter below we shall consider that language about God is sometimes not literal, and we shall refer to the fact that God the Son joined himself to a creature in personal identity in the Incarnation. If there were no gray areas, there would be no point in this discussion at all. Still, the bottom line is that for the Christian theologian there are clear standards as to what may and what may not be said. Some descriptions of God in the literature of the mystics are simply out of bounds in terms of Christian truth. The nature of the biblical God is not consistent with any and all properties.

The need for reconciliation. The writer of a mystery novel may point to a clue and subtly alert the reader that it will play an important role in the solution of the murder toward the end of the novel. In the same spirit I can mention here that the Christian doctrine of reconciliation is going to be of crucial importance in a later evaluation of mysticism. In their natural condition, human beings are not only finite but also sinful. They cannot stand in a positive relationship to God apart from the redemptive work of Christ, which becomes personal by faith. Any mystical system that loses sight of this reality cannot be incorporated into Christianity. It will become apparent that many Christian mystics must stand chastened at this point of their theology. They have a severely truncated understanding of their salvation, which is frequently equated with their mystical experience. But perhaps this understanding results from a simultaneously inadequate view of God and of scriptural authority. These matters must be argued out in detail below.

Methodological Presuppositions

A third set of presuppositions is methodological. They are largely implied by the fact that one would even set out on this inquiry, but they bear expressing once. Clearly there is something that we call mysticism. It is a reality, at least as an item of human belief and experience.[8]

Along this line, I need to presuppose that the best authority on the phenomena of mysticism are mystics themselves. It is their testimony that lets us know that there even is such a thing, and what it is like. It simply will not do to decide in advance what mystics experience. If they tell it one way, then all the scholarly treatises in the libraries cannot change that fact and somehow make them experience it some other way.

In the previous section we considered a number of theological presuppositions. These a priori convictions are crucial in only two specific ways. First, we may say to mystics that what they experienced, they should not have experienced (in the ethical sense of "should"). Perhaps their experiences are ones that no good Christian ought to have, and we could point that out to them. But such an exhortation would not change the actual mystical experience. Second, we may debate with mystics the interpretation of their experience. Insofar as they can distinguish between the experience and its interpretation (not at all a clear distinction, as we shall see), it is only the latter about which others may comment. The pure phenomenality of the experienced has to go unassailed.

One immediate consequence of such an open attitude is that we cannot reduce the mystical experience to any other experience. Stace rightly takes Bertrand Russell to task for looking at mystical experiences as nothing more than a set of emotions.[9] But we also need to be careful not to overemphasize what William James calls the "noetic quality of the

[8]Speaking theologically once more, I am not prepared to dismiss a priori the whole range of mystical experiences as the work of Satan. If I were convinced that this whole subject matter were occult, I would never have begun this project. Given my evangelical commitments, I believe that specific cases of mystical experiences may include real demonic influence. But that much, alas, can be said of many other religious activities—including superficially Christian ones.

[9]Stace, *Mysticism and Philosophy*, 14–15.

experience, viz. that it is a state of knowledge."[10] For, granting that there is a cognitive dimension, it certainly would still be inaccurate to call the whole experience cognitive. It is best to leave things uncategorized for now, with the assumption that mystical experience represents a genre of its own.

But with this observation we have now passed from the realm of preliminaries to the actual subject matter. It is high time to begin by defining our terms and stating what mysticism actually is. Let the inquiry begin.

---

[10]William James, *The Varieties of Religious Experience* (New York: Collier, 1961), 300.

2

What Is Mysticism?

THE READER WHO HAS WORKED THROUGH THE IN-troductory chapter now has earned the right to be given a clear definition of what mysticism is. But one who attempts such a definition finds oneself in a quandary. Already at the very early part of this discussion theoretical barriers arise.

The question concerns whether it is even possible to give a valid definition for all of mysticism or mysticism in general. Carl A. Keller, for example, has suggested that "it would perhaps be wise to avoid speaking of mysticism at all." For him, "it is a word devoid of concrete meaning."[1]

Such a prohibition leaves us with four options. First, we could simply ignore it, which would be poor scholarship. Second, we could try not to define mysticism, which would be as problematic as it would be unhelpful. For even Keller makes his modest proposal in an article on mystical literature in a book on mysticism. Surely he has an idea of what the term means. Third, we could now devote a chapter to the question of the possibility of there being a universal core of mysticism. Then the poor reader who is not yet versed in mysticism would need to plow through another lengthy discussion without being clear on the meaning of the subject.

---

[1]Carl A. Keller, "Mystical Literature," in *Mysticism and Philosophical Analysis*, ed. Steven T. Katz (New York: Oxford University Press, 1978), 96.

Fourth, we could now present a general statement on mysticism and then defend the making of such a general statement in the next chapter. Even though this fourth option may be methodologically odd, we proceed with it here.

Short Definitions

As happens with so many concepts one might try to define, many definitions will tend to be so specific as to say too much or so general as to say too little. In the first case, not all types of mysticism will be represented fairly; in the second case, none of them are represented fairly. Nonetheless we shall examine a few of them for their instructional value. However, the reader ought not to expect the miracle of an accurate, all-encompassing definition here.[2]

Lawrence J. Hatab gives us the following definition of mysticism: "The mystical is the decentralization of ego-consciousness, or, experience no longer centered in ego-consciousness." He defends this broad and highly negative definition because he believes this feature to constitute "the only thing all forms of mystical experience have in common."[3] If so, then different mystical experiences may at times have nothing significant in common, for statements about shared negatives may be only trivially true. All entities in the world, except marmosets, share the property of not-being-a-marmoset. But if I describe the Washington Monument by pointing out that it is not a marmoset, I am merely mouthing banalities. Similarly, if someone tries to give a definition for

[2]The possible objection that I cannot know what a term means unless I can provide an exhaustive definition for it rests on a thorough misunderstanding of the nature of language. We do not know what words mean because we know their definitions. Such a requirement would mean that all nonreflective language users (e.g. children) do not know the meaning of their talk—an absurd proposal. Surely definitions are quite helpful, e.g. when looking up the meaning of unknown words in dictionaries. But dictionaries also only report meaning; they do not legislate it.

[3]Lawrence J. Hatab, "Mysticism and Language,"*International Philosophical Quarterly* 22 (1982): 51.

all flight craft (airplanes, rockets, helicopters, etc.), one may state that the thing they all have in common is that they do not normally move on wheels. True enough, but we have not heard much about flight craft. Alternatively, we also see by way of the last example that negative definitions can open the door to greater misunderstandings. Other things, such as dogsleds and rowboats, also move without wheels.

Hatab's definition bears a similar flaw. His definition of mysticism unfortunately echoes the disintegration of ego-consciousness that is common for some mental illnesses but that we do not want to categorize with mysticism. In short, what Hatab points to is a very significant feature of mystical experience. The ordinary consciousness of ego is somehow dissolved in mysticism. But as a definition it will not suffice. Of course these criticisms of Hatab's definition do not reflect on the quality of his work in his article, which is knowledge-able and competent. Rather we are using Hatab's sophisticated definition as an illustration of the difficulty of coming up with an acceptable definition of mysticism.

Similar problems beset many of the positive definitions, such as Evelyn Underhill's "the apprehension of Reality."[4] Were it not for the obvious hidden agenda in this expression, as signaled by the capital R, this definition would be totally empty. As it is, it addresses only the initiated.

The problem is that if we try to be more specific, it is almost inescapable that we will simply make a hidden agenda public; that is, we will formulate a definition that is preju-diced toward a particular tradition. So, for example, D. D. Martin begins his dictionary article on mysticism with the tentative definition: "an experienced, direct, nonabstract, unmediated knowing of God, a knowing or seeing so direct as to be called union with God."[5] This definition is clearer than the previous two; one actually learns something about what

[4]Evelyn Underhill, *The Mystic Way: A Psychological Study in Christian Origins* (New York: Dutton, 1913).

[5]D. D. Martin, "Mysticism," in *Evangelical Dictionary of Theology*, ed. Walter Elwell (Grand Rapids: Baker, 1984), 744.

mysticism is supposed to be. However, initial enthusiasm may fade when one recognizes that Martin has deliberately limited himself to a definition of Christian mysticism, for mysticism outside of Christianity would be defined quite differently.

Nonetheless, with the aforementioned recognition that no definition is completely adequate, we can see in Martin's definition some general elements that do fit the general mystical pattern. The following summary by Marvin Kohl, which is certainly not a pure definition, sets the stage pretty well for understanding mysticism.

> There is an element of mystery in the universe (something which defies but also intrigues understanding) which cannot be reached by the usual modes of sensory experience; and this mystery is of the utmost significance for mankind. A mystic, therefore, is someone who either believes in, or experiences, an element of mystery in the universe which cannot be reached by the usual modes of sensory experience and to whom the belief or experience is of such significance that the individual structures an activity of his life in its expression or evaluation.[6]

To take this definition as summary would be controversial. Many a mystic—for example a Zen Buddhist—might take exception with these statements. But, in general, if one keeps this sort of pattern in mind, one is not likely to go wrong in too many specific cases of identifying and understanding mysticism.

Kohl's descriptive definition points out something else. It is becoming increasingly clear that to state what mysticism is all about, one has to tell something of a story, a description of human beings in the universe and how they relate to what is really important. Let us now pursue this avenue in the hope of coming to understand mysticism.

---

[6]Marvin Kohl, "The Unanimity Argument and the Mystics," *Hibbert Journal* 58 (1959): 275.

The Story of Mysticism

It should be apparent by now that the word "mysticism," as used in this study, refers to something other than what in common parlance is called mystical. It is perfectly legitimate in everyday speech to use the word "mystical" for any of the following: an unexplained or unexplainable event, something supernatural, a premonition, a miracle, or a vision. But among students of mysticism in the technical sense, the word refers to a rather specific phenomenon, as has been seen already.

This meaning of the word was not part of the origin of the word. It is derived from the ancient mystery religions, in which a certain insight was reserved only for the initiated. F. C. Happold explains that "the word 'mystery' *(mysterion)* comes from the Greek word *muō*, to shut or close the lips or eyes."[7] Thus the mystic is someone who is privy to wisdom closed to others. But we must not make the common mistake of determining the meaning of a word from its etymology (which Happold actually does not do).

Happold divides the story of mysticism into four points. For the sake of clarity we can break them up further into subpoints.

1. The nature of reality
   a. There is a "Divine Ground" which is true reality.
   b. The phenomenal world is only partial reality.
2. The nature of knowledge
   a. Human beings can have knowledge of the Divine Ground by inference.
   b. They can also have knowledge of the Divine Ground by a direct intuition, which is superior to all inferential knowledge.
3. The nature of human beings
   a. The human person consists of two selves.

---

[7]F. C. Happold, *Mysticism: A Study and an Anthology* (Baltimore: Penguin Books, 1963), 18.

   b. The phenomenal ego as daily existence is not the true self.
   c. The true self is an inner spiritual self that has either the same or a similar nature to the Divine Ground.
   d. By identifying with one's true self, a human being can identify with the Divine Ground.
 4. The purpose of human existence
   a. Human beings ought to identify with their true selves.
   b. Through this realization they identify with the Divine Ground and come to know pure Truth.
   c. Through this experience, the human being "will enter into a state of being which has been given different names, eternal life, salvation, enlightenment, etc."[8]

Let us resist the temptation immediately to launch into several criticisms that present themselves not only from the standpoints of theology and philosophy but also as a summary of mysticism. We have chapters ahead in which we can hone what is said here, and surely much cleaning up needs to be done. Nonetheless, most of what one normally encounters under the technical label "mysticism" can be seen to fit (or to be forced into) this general scheme. At the heart of all of mysticism lies some way of linking up with something absolute. Let us now look at some of the concepts brought up by Happold, but with a little more detail and in a slightly different sequence.

The Nature of Reality

The significance of mysticism's ontology lies in its commitment to something absolute. This absolute can be God; it can also be something abstract, nature, the cosmos, the totality of being, or even everyday reality (as in Zen). In each case this absolute is seen as the ultimate reference point.

---

[8]Ibid., 20.

It may be understood as the only reality (Brahman in Vedanta Hinduism) or as the source of all reality (God in Christianity). The absolute can be contrasted with something nonabsolute: Brahman distinguished from maya, God held distinct from creation and so forth. In cases such as Zen, where common reality itself takes on the role of the absolute, the distinction has to be made between looking at reality as self-contained and given or seeing reality as questionable, contingent, and metaphysically dependent.

It may be helpful here to draw on Rudolf Otto's distinction between extrovertive and introvertive mysticism.[9] The experience of extrovertive mystics consists essentially of seeing something outside of themselves as absolute. Introvertive mystics, on the other hand, look inside of themselves and find there at the bottom of their very self the final truth. They may then equate this self with God (e.g. Atman-Brahman in Hinduism), but this equation may be a secondary inference. The self is the absolute.

We must be careful in this general description to leave the term "absolute" as neutral as possible. Happold's phrase "Divine Ground" already begs the question in favor of a religious conception. Such a bias would be even more evident if we called it God, but also if we referred to it as something transcendent, True Reality, the One, or any such term. The "absolute" (which I am deliberately not capitalizing) can be any of those things; the absoluteness consists primarily of its irrefragability as reference point. Thus the expression is as much epistemological (having to do with the order of knowing) as metaphysical (having to do with reality). But this absolute is in some sense the most crucial reality. It should be clear that it makes little difference for this scheme if the absolute reality is nothingness (e.g. sunyata of Buddhism). It is only necessary that this nothingness be the absolute reference point.

---

[9]Rudolf Otto, *Mysticism East and West* (New York: Collier, 1960).

The Nature of the Self

Not much can be said in a general way that would be true of every mystic's conception of the self. Happold's dichotomy between the phenomenal self and the true self (ego and self; Hindu *jiva* and *atman*) is applicable in many mystical systems, but not in others where the self is seen as a plain entity. Nor is it necessary to stipulate that the mystical experience concerns the nature of the self, let alone that the self is always somehow identical to the absolute.

But one thing is clear for all of mysticism: At its core is the human individual who experiences himself or herself in relationship to the absolute. Mysticism is not merely a set of metaphysical truths, nor would a corporate mysticism be usually recognizable as such unless it was accompanied by the mysticism of the individual members constituting a group. Again we need to avoid becoming too specific, but it is very hard to envision a mysticism that is not centered on individuals and their particular experiences.

The Link to the Absolute

Continuing to tread carefully, we can now touch on a third crucial phase within mysticism, namely, the context of the mystical experience as an unmediated link between the person and the absolute. Happold speaks of knowledge in which knower and known are united, and even of identity of the person and the absolute. This conception is one (perhaps an extreme) version of the link exemplified in Vedantic Hinduism among other traditions. But this understanding would again be far too narrow for all of mysticism. The link need not be identity; it could be a unity of will or purpose, an absorption, a mutual embracing, or a direct vision—just so long as there is direct, unmediated contact.

Speaking of visions, we need to clarify that simply having a vision or audition might not qualify as technically mystical unless it was an experience that consisted of some direct contact with the absolute. In other words, if I had a vision of St. Boniface, that experience might not be truly mystical (though it would be strange, unusual, and supernatural), but a vision of Christ, who is my God, would be.

This unmediated link, whatever its specific nature, clearly exceeds normal human experience. To be more specific, the experience of the link is (1) not merely the exercise of one of our usual faculties (e.g. sight or reason); (2) not usually thought of as something a majority of people experience; (3) not even always a part of the experience of all of the members of the religious group in which a particular mystical strand may have originated. Thus not every Taoist has had a Taoist mystical experience; not every Christian has had a Christian mystical experience, and so forth. Frequently mystics will consider the experience of this unmediated link to be the highest possible human experience, for it permits the maximum contact with the absolute as allowed by their particular tradition.

The Experience

The story of mysticism is incomplete apart from the element of the experience in which the link to the absolute is realized. We still can speak only in the most general terms, but for many practical surveys of mysticism, the very categories of mysticism and mystical experience are synonymous. And yet we may do well to add a qualifier at this juncture and point out a certain asymmetry. As hinted already, certain kinds of preternatural experiences not in the context of the points of this section should best not be considered mysticism in the technical sense. At the same time, we need to hold the door open to a system of thought embodying those points that does not demand a specific experience but that is nonetheless properly called a mystical system. Kiekhefer has called this possibility a mysticism of "habitual union."[10]

---

[10]Richard Kiekhefer, "Meister Eckhart's Conception of Union with God," *Harvard Theological Review* 71 (1978): 204.

Despite the perpetual problem of attempting to do justice to every tradition, certain writers have isolated the most crucial features of mystical experience. William James has singled out four characteristics.[11] In first place he puts "ineffability," the fact that the nature of the experience cannot be directly communicated with language. Second, he mentions "noetic quality," by which he means that mystics believe that in some sense they have received knowledge during their experience. These two characteristics, as paradoxical as they may seem taken together, are actually already sufficient to constitute a mystical experience according to James.

But James adds two other characteristics that further describe mystical experience. These are "transciency" and "passivity," which indicate that the experience is usually short-lived and not entirely within the control of the individual having it.

It must be emphasized that what James is trying to give here is an objective—almost clinical—description of the experience itself, not the beliefs or interpretations that provide the framework for the experience (note the discussion above of the nature of reality, the nature of the self, and the link to the absolute). Whether such an endeavor is successful or even possible remains to be seen.

A similar observation needs to accompany the seven-point list given by W. T. Stace.[12] In the first two he distinguishes between the extrovertive and introvertive mystical experiences.

1. Oneness (for the extrovertive type, this means seeing all things as one; in the introvertive type, the experience is of unitary pure consciousness).
2. The characteristics of oneness (extrovertive: inner subjectivity in all things; introvertive: nonspatial, nontemporal).

---

[11]James, *Varieties*, 299–300.
[12]Stace, *Mysticism and Philosophy*, 131–33.

3. Sense of objectivity or reality.
4. Feeling of blessedness, peace, etc.
5. Feeling of the holy, sacred, or divine.
6. Paradoxicality.
7. Alleged ineffability.

Stace has placed James's first and most important characteristic, ineffability, in last place. He qualifies it with the words "alleged by mystics," and he also says that he is adding this characteristic "with reservations."[13] Some of the reasons for James's enthusiasm for this characteristic will become apparent when we examine ineffability per se in chapter 5. But some of the difference here may lie in the fact that Stace is already interpreting more than James. Whereas James simply takes the mystic's claim of ineffability at face value, Stace wants to remain open to the possibility that, even though mystics allege ineffability, the experience is actually not beyond language. However, if one wants to adopt a purely phenomenological attitude toward the mystical experience, then Stace's reservations are unnecessary.

To summarize the nature of the mystical experience, two important characteristics stand out among all of the ones that have been or could be listed. First, it is an experience of unity. However the link between human and absolute may be conceived, in this experience the link is felt to be closed. Frequently there is a feeling of absolute oneness, as mentioned by Stace, though we cannot insist that all proper mystical experiences include this aspect.

Second, it needs to be underscored, despite the apparent controversy, that mystics do not believe that their experience is entirely rational. They do not see their connection with the absolute as coming through either their reason or their senses directly. As a consequence, it is typical for the mystic to claim that his or her experience is beyond normal rational categories. It cannot be grasped by reason, let alone explained with language, which relies on our rational faculties. Leaving aside

---

[13]Ibid., 79.

the question of whether this fact allows us to state dogmatically that all mystical experience is ineffable, it is certainly neither a rational nor a linguistic and conceptual experience.

As a last remark on the nature of this experience, we need to distance ourselves critically from Happold's analysis. We may grant that the experience is always extremely important to the mystic. But it would be a serious mistake always to expect the experience to be at the center of the mystic's faith; and it is certainly not always a mystic's understanding of the goal and purpose of life. Consider, for example, the idea of equating the mystical experience with salvation in those contexts where it is a relevant concept. Some mystics do believe that their salvation lies in their experience. But many other representatives can be found for whom mystical experience, though significant, is not as important as their state of salvation. Recall here Kiekhefer's idea of habitual union, which denies the need for an experience altogether.

We can incorporate all of the above observations into one short summary of typical mysticism: *The mystic believes that there is an absolute and that he or she can enjoy an unmediated link to this absolute in a superrational experience.* Such a statement is almost too empty to say anything definite. Certainly there are many philosophical and theological issues begging for clarification, which we will consider in subsequent chapters. For now, it is best to add some flesh to the skeleton and give a few examples of mysticism.

A Few Examples

The following brief examples are provided only to illustrate the previous discussion. I am not claiming that in some way these examples are "typical," which would involve the dubious implication that there could be "less typical" instances. It follows, then, that we also are not surveying the major classifications of mysticism, though these examples are deliberately chosen because they differ markedly from each other.

Also, in the light of the foregoing discussion, it would not be helpful now to quote reports from various mystics of their experiences. It will be much more significant for our purposes to summarize the settings in which mystical experiences are reported to occur.

Vedanta

A very clear representation of mysticism is found in the phase of Indian religion called Vedantic (the Vedanta is a supplement to the Vedas, the Hindu holy scriptures). The Vedantic scriptures, the Upanishads, represent a reaction to the religion of the Vedas, which was a religion of ritual, centering on the sacrificial rites performed by the official priests, the Brahmins. The heart of the Upanishadic message is that true reality is found beyond the empty repetitions of actions and words of the ritual.[14]

The Upanishads claim that there is one reality beyond all appearances. This is Brahman, the supreme being (*sat*, sometimes referred to as *tat*), for it is beyond all categories of thought and speech. Brahman is all and beyond all. It is found everywhere, and yet it cannot be located in any one space.[15]

The phenomenal world is not Brahman as such. It is maya, the magical projection of Brahman, perhaps better translated as "appearance" than as the more common "illusion." It is the playful manifestation of Brahman, real as maya, but not ultimately real. Maya encompasses not only the external world but also human beings in their physical, psychological, and even religious dimensions.

But deep within oneself in a place that cannot be isolated, is the person's link to Brahman.[16] And this link is nothing

[14]J. N. Hattiangadi, "Why Is Indian Religion Mystical?" *Journal of Indian Philosophy* 3 (1975): 253–58.

[15]*Chandogya Upanishad* 6.1–3, 12–14, in William Theodore de Bary, *Sources of Indian Tradition*, 2 vols. (New York: Columbia University Press, 1958), 1:31–34.

[16]*Chandogya Upanishad*, 8.7–12; de Bary *Sources of Indian Tradition* 1:28–31.

short of true identity. Looking into one's innermost self, one discovers atman, which is in every respect Brahman. *Tat tvam asi!* (That are thou!) is the bottom line of the Upanishads.[17]

Thus the goal of the religion becomes realization of this identity. Nothing has to be done or even could be done to bring it about; it is reality already. In fact it is the most fundamental aspect of the universe. Thus Vedantic mysticism does not usually recommend a certain experience as the gateway into truth. Although it may include a mystical experience as described above, the Upanishads themselves do not make the experience the prerequisite for the Atman-Brahman identity. But the realization of truth may come packaged with the recognizable mystical traits as found in James and Stace. The Self (Atman-Brahman) "is not knowable by perception, turned inward or outward, nor by both combined. He is neither that which is known, nor that which is not known, nor is He the sum of all that might be known. He cannot be seen, grasped, bargained with. He is undefinable, unthinkable, indescribable."[18]

St. John of the Cross

The writings of St. John of the Cross present a rhapsodic description of how to attain and enjoy mystical experience within the Christian thought of sixteenth-century Spain.[19] Together with Teresa of Avila, John spearheaded monastic reform based on severe discipline within the Carmelite order. He advocated mystical union as the pinnacle of Christian experience.

John elaborated extensively on the classic three stages that are supposed to comprise the mystical way. First there is the way of purgation. The adept needs to remove all sin from his or her life, both internal and external. Only one who is truly pure may go on to greater heights of spirituality. John

---

[17]*Chandogya Upanishad*, 6.12–14.
[18]*Mandocky Upanishad*, cited in Happold, *Mysticism*, 146–47.
[19]Happold, *Mysticism*, 355–66.

called the often painful process of purgation the "dark night of the soul."[20]

The way of purgation is followed by the way of illumination. Here one attempts to do two things: come to know genuine spiritual truth, and abstract oneself from all hindrances of this life. Counted among the obstacles are even conventional religious concepts.

Finally there is the way of union. Now the soul attains oneness with God. John describes this union in terms of spiritual betrothal, where the soul, conceived of as feminine, is married to Christ as the bridegroom.[21] In other places he may say things that sound almost Vedantic ("The centre of the soul is God"),[22] but it is clear that he does not mean to advocate a unity based on a given identity so much as a union brought about as two lovers unite. The two become one. Love motivates the union, and the union should be sought only as the product of the love, not for the ecstasy of the experience.

Black Elk

A very different kind of mysticism can be found in the experience of Black Elk, a Sioux medicine man who was alive at the time of Custer's defeat at Little Big Horn and who related his story to John G. Neihardt in the 1930s.[23]

As a nine-year-old child, Black Elk had a "power vision" that shaped his entire life. In this big and complex vision he was transported into the sky, where he was presented with many apocalyptic pictures and messages. Although we do not want to consider visions as mystical per se, Black Elk's power

---

[20]St. John of the Cross, "The Ascent of Mount Carmel," 1, 1 and 2, in Happold, *Mysticism*, 358–59.

[21]St. John of the Cross, "The Spiritual Canticle," 14, in Happold, *Mysticism*, 363.

[22]St. John of the Cross, "The Living Flame of Love," 1, in Happold, *Mysticism*, 362.

[23]John G. Neihardt, *Black Elk Speaks: Being the Life Story of a Holy Man of the Oglala Sioux* (New York: Pocket Books, 1932).

vision is most important for us because it set the agenda for his later spiritual experiences.

Black Elk moved into adolescence a sickly and sensitive boy. Slowly he grew into warriorhood through the events of his day—the wars, the sufferings, the victory at Little Big Horn, and the subsequent sojourn in Canada. But as he grew, so did his fear of the spiritual world. He was particularly terrified by the thunder beings of the West.

When Black Elk's condition had reached a particularly serious point, his case came to the attention of a medicine man named Black Road. Upon investigation, Black Road decided that Black Elk needed to act out his vision in a dance, called the horse dance. On the appointed day, with the help of many people of the tribe, everything was prepared for the dance. The tepee was decorated with illustrations from the vision. Inside the tepee six men sat representing the Six Grandfathers. Other recruits included men to ride groups of horses of various colors, and four virgins. Then every phase of Black Elk's vision was acted out. Black Elk himself carried a red stick representing the sacred arrow of the thunder beings and sang the songs that had been taught him in his vision.

The horse dance ended with the ceremonial smoking of the pipe. Afterward Black Elk was a changed person. "After the horse dance was over, it seemed that I was above the ground and did not touch it when I walked. . . . The fear that was on me so long was gone, and when thunder clouds appeared I was always glad to see them for they came as relatives now to visit me. Everything seemed good and beautiful now, and kind."[24] From this point on he grew spiritually and soon was able to perform healings—he had become a medicine man.

Black Elk's mysticism is certainly very different from the mystical way of St. John of the Cross or Vedantic metaphysics. Nonetheless, even here we can see a basic pattern. Black Elk too established an unmediated link to his conception of the

---

[24]Ibid., 147–48.

absolute. The horse dance was the means to bring about the contact between Black Elk and his "relatives," the thunder beings.

An Anonymous Cabalist

Gershom Sholem has reproduced for us a document coming out of the cabalistic school of Abraham Abulafia. In general, we can say that at the heart of Jewish mysticism lies *devekuth*, which is literally "adherence" to God. In the various schools of Jewish mysticism, this notion is given very different construals and may be brought about in many different ways. The school of Abraham Abulafia distinguished itself by focusing attention on the name of God as the way to attain bliss.[25]

An anonymous disciple of Abulafia's, possibly in Palestine, described the experience. He had spent quite a bit of time studying the Torah and the Talmud, but without much excitement. Explorations in the philosophy of Moses Maimonides added to his intellectual knowledge but did not contribute greatly to his spirituality. Then his teacher suggested to him that he try out the mysteries of the cabala.

The teacher introduced him to the techniques of combining letters, particularly the letters that make up the names of God, in various ways. This the disciple began to practice, along with a general withdrawal from the world. One night, as he was manipulating letters, he dozed off; upon awaking, he realized that he was aglow.

The disciple continued to undertake exercises with the letters of the Hebrew alphabet. One night the letters suddenly started to arrange themselves pretty much on their own, and they grew in size. The disciple trembled and became so weak that he fell down; something like speech moved from his heart to his lips. This phenomenon occurred each time he worked

---

[25]Gershom G. Sholem, *Major Trends in Jewish Mysticism* (New York: Schocken, 1941), 147–55, 133.

on the "Great Name of God." After he built up his spiritual strength, he was able to undertake this experimentation without ill effect, but when he started to manipulate the letters *YHWH*, he heard a voice condemn him to death. Nevertheless, he pleaded with God to spare him on the strength of his pure motive: wanting only to know God. At this point he had his overwhelming experience. "And behold, I was still speaking and oil like the oil of the anointment anointed me from head to foot and very great joy seized me which for its spirituality and the sweetness of its rapture I cannot describe."[26]

In many ways, Jewish mysticism is very conservative. There is no talk here of identity between God and the human searcher, or even of direct union. Other schools make much greater claims. However, even here we see this cabalistic adept having a direct encounter with God on the basis of combining and permutating the letters of God's name.

F. C. Happold

Sometimes the bare mystical experience is presented as though it occurred apart from any story or metaphysical context. F. C. Happold attempts to create this impression, when in his anthology on mysticism he reproduces the earlier account of his own mystical experiences.[27]

As a young man at Cambridge, Happold had the experience of a "Presence" in his room with him, which filled him with an overwhelming and lasting joy. A similar experience somewhat later was accompanied by a voice speaking a paradoxical message. Twice later in life, at the eve of a World War I battle and immediately prior to the birth of his child, Happold received a feeling of absolute and unconditioned security.

Happold describes these experiences as having occurred

---

[26]Ibid., 152.

[27]F. C. Happold, "Adventure in Search of a Creed," in Happold, *Mysticism*, 133–35.

prior to having a conceptual apparatus for accommodating them. He states, "Though I now recognize the experience as of the kind described by the mystics, at that time I knew nothing of mysticism." But all this statement says is that Happold later on acquired a philosophical vocabulary with which to analyze his experience as a sort of second-order explanation. When he started to commit himself to the idea of mysticism in general, he dismissed his earlier attempts to understand the experience. He tells us, for example, that at first he likened his experience to a "vision of the Holy Grail."[28] Later on, he decided that the vocabulary of the perennial philosophy was more adequate in making sense out of what happened to him. But such is not to say that the experiences first occurred totally without prior conceptual commitment.

It may not be unfair to suggest that such analysis could be done successfully with most other accounts of supposed mystical experiences prior to understanding of a mystical system. In most cases, a little digging will reveal a prior commitment to the context into which the mystical experience is eventually absorbed. St. John of the Cross was not suddenly struck by a Vedantic mystical experience, and Black Elk did not suddenly dream about the marriage of his soul to Christ. Just so Happold, as well as many others who have similar stories to tell, had their original experience in the light of their absolutes at the time, subsequent reexplanation notwithstanding.

In this chapter we have suggested a core definition of mysticism as a personal, unmediated link to an absolute and have attempted to provide a general framework within which mysticism can be understood. But we have left open the question of whether such a general framework truly represents a universal core of mysticism, let alone whether there is such a core at all. We take up this question in the next chapter.

---

[28]Ibid., 134, 133.

3

Does Mysticism Have a Common Core?

ANY STUDY OF MYSTICISM MUST ASK WHETHER IT IS legitimate to treat mysticism as a unified phenomenon. We have defined mysticism as an unmediated link to an absolute, thereby apparently assuming that there are certain characteristics that all mysticism possesses. But such a supposition is highly questionable. Many important writers today have argued that mysticism has no unifying core. Writers have taken four positions on this issue.[1]

1. All forms of mysticism are manifestations of basic mysticism. Essentially all of mysticism, apart from purely verbal distinctions, is of one cloth.
2. All forms of mysticism should be manifestations of basic mysticism, but some deviate from the norm. Thus there could be a contrast between pure and adulterated mysticism.
3. It is legitimate to classify certain types of mysticism into distinctive categories. Thus there is a possible finite number of basic forms of mysticism.
4. There is no basic mysticism apart from each unique case of mysticism. We cannot find a common core or

[1]See Steven T. Katz, "Language, Epistemology, and Mysticism," in *Mysticism and Philosophical Analysis*, ed. Steven T. Katz (New York: Oxford University Press, 1978), 23–24.

broader categories, and we should not attempt to impose a unifying structure or categorization on the specific forms.

In the literature, the distinctions are often more blurred than they appear in this delineation. For example, researchers may advocate position 1, the unanimity of mysticism. But confronted with apparently differing data, they may eventually resort to the prescriptivism of position 2 and simply rule out some form of mysticism as nonstandard or even improper. Since these two positions do go hand in hand more often than not, I shall generally treat them together.

Advocates of Unanimity

In *The Perennial Philosophy*, Aldous Huxley attempted to show by way of excerpted quotations that many mystics say identical things.[2] But it may be in his *Doors of Perception* that he makes his strongest theoretical case for the essential sameness of mystical forms. Huxley stipulates a mental function that he calls the "Mind-at-Large." This Mind-at-Large is the human capacity for transcending usual cerebral processes and thereby even the self. An accepted form of self-transcendence is religion, which, however, may not work for everyone. He states, "Ideally, everyone should be able to find self-transcendence in some form of pure or applied religion. In practice it seems unlikely that this hoped for consummation will ever be realized."[3]

But if religious self-transcendence is not attained, it becomes just as legitimate in Huxley's view to use drugs to achieve the same goal. "The urge to transcend self-conscious selfhood is, as I have said, a principal appetite of the soul. When, for whatever reason, men and women fail to transcend themselves by means of worship, good works and spiritual

[2]Aldous Huxley, *The Perennial Philosophy* (Cleveland: World, 1962).
[3]Aldous Huxley, *The Doors of Perception* (New York: Harper and Row, 1954), 68.

exercises, they are apt to resort to religion's chemical surrogates." In fact, Huxley goes so far as to wish to mandate that thinking people be subjected to a chemical experience of transcendence.[4] As long as some form of transcendence is achieved, the means of bringing it about are irrelevant. Huxley can maintain such a stance only if he believes that all forms of self-transcendence (i.e. mysticism) are inherently the same.

Such is also the attitude of F. C. Happold, who makes the questionable statement that "mysticism has manifested itself in similar or identical forms wherever the mystical consciousness has been present."[5] Happold asserts that there is a mysticism and a mystical consciousness that make themselves known. And when they do, they appear in hardly indistinguishable forms.

That Happold considers the differences among forms of mysticism to be superficial only is also illustrated by a statement he makes in introducing a number of case studies in mystical experience. He says, "A reading of them may, perhaps, convince the reader of the relevance of mysticism to himself."[6] In other words, behind the invitation to consider the specific forms of mysticism, there is the broader lure of mysticism per se.

This point of view becomes most interesting when one tries to isolate the nature or essential properties of mysticism in general. What actually counts as pure mysticism? Can it be uncovered in every single mystical instance? Happold gives four basic characteristics of mystical experience (divine ground, direct intuition of the divine, true self, identity).[7]

---

[4]Ibid., 68, 78.

[5]Happold, *Mysticism*, 20. On p. 118 Happold denies the "oneness" of mystical experience but then asserts that the unanimity of the mystics is found "at a deeper level." I think he means simply that mystics have different conceptual descriptions for their experiences but that there is a common ground behind them all.

[6]Ibid., 129.

[7]Ibid., 20.

Similarly Stace, as we have seen, listed seven characteristics common to all mystical experience.[8]

But Stace makes a remarkable assertion in the context of identifying the mystical core. For he is aware that such a core cannot be demonstrated in every instance of mysticism. So he makes the judgment that some forms belong to the group that might manifest the core and others simply do not. "There will be a central nucleus of typical cases which are typical because they share an important set of common characteristics. But there will be borderline cases."[9] The irony is that what separates the two groups is nothing more than Stace's own standard of what constitutes the so-called important characteristics that supposedly make an experience "typical."

In a sharp criticism of such methodology, Marvin Kohl states,

> This . . . technique is alarmingly simple. One simply states that "X" is a definition of true mysticism. "X" of course, specifies certain beliefs as to the nature of a Supreme Being. Those who do not conform to this criterion are not true mystics. Those who do conform are true mystics and are in almost unanimous agreement as to his nature. The philosopher then appears and proudly points to this unanimity as evidence of their knowledge of the Divine. It is obvious, I think, that such a technique is nothing more than a form of begging the question.[10]

To support this accusation, Kohl points to Bergson, W. R. Inge, and Evelyn Underhill as examples.[11] These all argue for the unanimity of the mystic witness only after they have eliminated the testimony of all but those whom they have deemed "pure" mystics.[12]

---

[8]Stace, *Mysticism and Philosophy*, 131–32.
[9]Ibid., 46.
[10]Kohl, "Unanimity Argument," 275.
[11]Henri Bergson, *The Two Sources of Morality and Religion* (Garden City, N.Y.: Doubleday Anchor, 1935), 246–47; William Ralph Inge, *Christian Mysticism* (New York: Scribner's, 1933), vii; Evelyn Underhill, *Mysticism* (New York: Dutton, 1911), 104.
[12]Kohl, "Unanimity Argument," 272.

With this telling criticism, we are now armed to move on to the next section. For if the criticism is right (as I believe it is), then there must be at least a finite number of different types of mysticism.

Classification into Categories

R. C. Zaehner has challenged Aldous Huxley on the question of unanimity.[13] He raises the question of whether it makes any sense at all to equate a drug–induced mysticism with a theistic mysticism. For example, can one reasonably maintain that Huxley's statement of "being my Not-self in the Not-self which was the chair," generated by a dose of mescaline, is somehow the equivalent of the raptures of the soul in union with Christ as described by St. John of the Cross?

In pursuing Zaehner's argument, we can consider here Stace's principle of causal indifference, according to which the origin of an experience is irrelevant to its content.[14] This principle is highly dubious and certainly must be rejected, since it is hard to imagine what even could count as evidence for it. But Zaehner's argument, and the point of this section, is that Huxley's equivalence cannot be demonstrated, even with a principle of causal indifference. Some differences among forms of mysticism and the very experiences they are associated with are simply too significant to ignore.

Zaehner believes that he has identified three distinct categories of mysticism that ought not to be confounded with each other. First there is nature, or "pan-en-henic" mysticism. This type of mysticism is essentially natural in that it triggers an inherent mystical capacity within the person. Zaehner refers to the analytical psychologist C. G. Jung and his idea that a segment of the collective unconscious intrudes on the conscious mind. This idea would make the pan-en-henic state

---

[13]R. C. Zaehner, *Mysticism: Sacred and Profane* (London: Oxford University Press, 1957).

[14]Stace, *Mysticism and Philosophy*, 29–31.

seriously comparable to a psychosis.[15] And, of course, it can also be induced by drugs.

Zaehner's second category of mysticism is monistic mysticism. This type is exemplified by Hindu and Buddhist mysticism. The individual is here sublated into the impersonal All, whatever specific name one might give to it.

The third category is theistic mysticism. Here the absolute is a personal God and the relationship takes on personal qualities. For example, love for God becomes a dominant theme for Christian or Sufi mystics. Zaehner argues, "The [monist] achieves liberation entirely by his own efforts since there is no God apart from himself to help him or with whom he can be united. In the case of the theistic mystic, on the other hand, it is always God who takes the first step, and it is God who works in the soul and makes it fit for union." Zaehner's bottom line is simple: "Thus it seems that theist and monist cannot ever agree."[16] And what goes for these two groups would apply to them in relation to pan-en-henic mysticism a fortiori. Consequently one cannot confuse these types with each other, and we have three distinct categories of mysticism.

Or do we? Ninian Smart has questioned Zaehner's conclusion in an important article. His thesis is that "there is no essential distinction between what Zaehner has called monistic and theistic mysticism."[17] He attempts to support this claim with a sharp distinction between an experience and its interpretation.

Experience and Interpretation

The distinction that Smart advocates and refines has been invoked by many others in an attempt to isolate a core mystical experience. Stace has commented on Zaehner's classification.

---

[15]Zaehner, *Mysticism: Sacred and Profane*, 106.
[16]Ibid., 192, 206.
[17]Smart, "Interpretation," 88.

> The point is that Professor Zaehner's conclusion simply does not follow from the mere fact that the *beliefs* which Christian mystics based upon their experiences are different from the *beliefs* which the Indian based on theirs. And the difference of beliefs is really the only difference which he offers for his view. A genuine grasp of the distinction between experience and interpretation . . . might have resulted in a fuller, fairer, and more impartial examination and treatment of the two possible hypotheses.[18]

This critique stipulates that a basic experience is then interpreted by the subject, who has the experience in accordance with his or her beliefs. We already mentioned Stace's commitment to the view that a core mystical experience is common to all occurrences of (what he considers to be) typical mysticism. Now Zaehner has rightly pointed out that the mystic does not report a core experience, but union with God or identity with Brahman, and so forth. But Stace counters with the thesis that wherever the mystic's report exceeds the basic experience (as delineated by Stace), this excess is simply the mystic's own interpretation.

According to Stace, the experience itself is neutral to any belief group. Of course the mystics' reports are not neutral. Stace asserts, "The Christian mystic *usually says* that what he experiences is 'union with God.' The Hindu mystic *says* that his experience is one in which his individual self is identical with Brahman or the Universal Self."[19] However, the discerning philosopher is supposed to be able to see through what the mystics say and realize that the same essential experience has given rise to various interpretations.

Smart elaborates on this distinction by introducing two further parameters. First of all, he asks us to note how much the interpretation of an experience relies on other beliefs and concepts. He refers to an interpretation that involves a lot of other factors as being of "high ramification," whereas a fairly neutral interpretation that restricts itself as much as possible

---

[18]Stace, *Mysticism and Philosophy*, 36.
[19]Ibid., 34 (emphasis mine).

to a pure description of the experience is one of "low ramification." Furthermore, it is crucial to distinguish between the interpretation mystics themselves give of their experience from the interpretation given by others. Smart calls these the "auto-interpretation" and "hetero-interpretation" respectively.[20]

In this terminology a "low auto-interpretation" would mean that a mystic minimizes extraneous material in interpreting his or her experience. A "high hetero-interpretation" implies that someone else interprets the mystical experience by bringing in a lot of concepts from one's own extraneous set of beliefs. And this latter sin—high hetero-interpretation—is what Smart accuses Zaehner of.

Smart summarizes his own conclusions in three statements:

1. "Phenomenologically, mysticism is everywhere the same.
2. "Different flavours, however, accrue to the experiences of mystics because of their ways of life and modes of auto-interpretation.
3. "The truth of interpretation depends in large measure on factors extrinsic to the mystical experience itself."[21]

Thus we see here how Smart has somewhat refined the distinction between experience and interpretation in order to safeguard the idea of a core mystical experience. But this hallowed distinction has come under severe attack by Steven Katz and some of his coworkers.

Pluralism

In a later essay Ninian Smart has reiterated the position described above.[22] However, this later essay serves as a foil in a

---

[20]Smart, "Interpretation," 78–81.
[21]Ibid., 88.
[22]Ninian Smart, "Understanding Religious Experience," in *Mysticism and Philosophical Analysis*, ed. Steven T. Katz (New York: Oxford University Press, 1978), 10–21.

volume edited by Steven T. Katz that presents critical reactions to this point from various perspectives. Katz himself wrote a lengthy and definitive statement of the thesis.

Katz makes the point that experience is never concept-neutral. He informs us of the "single epistemological assumption that has exercised [his] thinking," namely, "there are no pure (i.e. unmediated) experiences." Thus he takes severe issue with the Stacian thesis of a neutral experience with subsequent interpretation.[23] But Katz goes further and also rejects Zaehner's handy division of mysticism into three types as inadequate. For Zaehner's own methodology should lead him to see that even within each of the types, there are various religious orientations that necessarily exclude each other. If we look at Zaehner's theistic mysticism, we discover a genuine pluralism of mystical forms.[24] According to Katz, "For example, both Jewish and Christian mystics are for the most part theistic in the broad sense, yet the experience of Jewish mystics is radically different from that met in Christian circles. And again the 'theism' of the Bhagavad Gita or of Ramanuja is markedly different from the theism of Teresa of Avila, Isaac Luria, or Al Hallaj."[25]

Thus Katz advances the thesis that a Hindu does not have an experience that is subsequently clothed in Hindu terms, but the Hindu has a Hindu experience. Of a Jewish mysticism he asserts that the "images, beliefs, symbols, and rituals define *in advance*, what the experience *he wants to have*, and which he does then have, will be like."[26] In other words, the beliefs and concepts that others classified under "interpreta-

---

[23]Katz, "Language, Epistemology, and Mysticism," 26, 30.

[24]Thus Zaehner sits in the unenviable position of being attacked from both sides: he has to fend off charges both of introducing distinctions where there are none and of not introducing a sufficient number of distinctions. If truth could be judged by being in the middle between two extremes, Zaehner would surely have to be right.

[25]Katz, "Language, Epistemology, and Mysticism," 32.

[26]Ibid., 26, 33.

tion of an experience," Katz considers to be constituents of the experience.[27]

One of Katz's main lines of defense (or attack) is to contrast two different mystical goals: the idea of "clinging to God" in Jewish mysticism (devekuth) and the extinction of all desires in Buddhism (nirvana). He then concludes: "Whatever nirvana is, and indeed whatever devekuth is, in so far as words mean anything and philosophical inquiry has any significance, there is no way one can describe, let alone equate, the experience of nirvana and devekuth on the basis of evidence."[28]

And again Katz reiterates that this analysis is not a matter of the Jew or the Buddhist simply interpreting their experiences differently but of different belief systems creating different experiences. Thus a "mystic brings to his experience a world of concepts, images, symbols, and values which shape as well as colour the experience which he eventually and actually has."[29]

But surely there must be evidence to the contrary as well. Huxley, Stace, and many other writers would not have argued for the perennial philosophy if there is none. The evidence is there, in fact, that mystics of many different backgrounds do say very similar things about their experiences, often using identical words.

Katz responds to this rejoinder by making a point from modern language philosophy. He states that "language is itself contextual and words 'mean' only in contexts."[30] In other

---

[27]This concept appears to be very similar to the function of intentionality in phenomenology. Here also, in a very real sense, the transcendental ego constitutes its own experience of the noemata by way of extending itself to it through intentionality. In this interpretation there is no neutral experience or bedrock object of experience apart from the subject's intentional grasp of the object in the experience.

[28]Katz, "Language, Epistemology, and Mysticism," 39. Note Katz's reply to someone who might wish to argue that perhaps words do not mean anything and philosophical inquiry might have no significance. In that case no position—neither a monism nor a pluralism—could be supported (40).

[29]Ibid., 46.

[30]Ibid., 47.

words, when two mystics from different traditions use the same words, those words do not mean the same thing because they occur in different contexts. Any similarity of language would be strictly accidental. No shared meaning can be inferred from the common use of one term.

Thus each form of mysticism is a universe to itself. There is no common core mystical experience. No one definition captures all of mysticism. There are no objective types of mysticism represented in various traditions. There are as many forms of mysticism as there are mystical traditions.[31]

Katz is not without support from other scholars in advocating his thesis. Bruce Garside had already stated the claim that the so-called interpretation of a mystical experience is part of the "set" that constitutes it. In this argument also, Smart's earlier distinction between levels of ramification seems unhelpful. "With the exception of a very few cases, it is a distortion to regard descriptions of mystical experiences as if they were interpretations."[32] Similarly, Jure Kristo has argued that "mystical experience is like all experience, conditioned by cultural, historical, philosophical, and religious presuppositions and assumptions."[33]

One of the strongest statements defending the Katz line on mystical pluralism can be found in an essay by Carl A. Keller, reproduced in the same volume with Katz's article. Keller counsels, "In order to avoid misunderstanding, it would perhaps be wise to avoid speaking of 'mysticism' at all." Keller recognizes that there have been many people in movements for a deeper spirituality, but, "they neither practiced nor propagated 'mysticism.'" Finally, then, Keller goes so far as to say, "Mysticism is an abstract concept. It is a word devoid of concrete meaning."[34]

---

[31]Ibid., 51.

[32]Bruce Garside, "Language and the Interpretation of Mystical Experience," *International Journal for Philosophy of Religion* 3 (1972): 101.

[33]Jure Kristo, "The Interpretation of Religious Experience: What Do Mystics Intend When They Talk about Their Experiences?" *Journal of Religion* 62 (1982): 21–38.

[34]Keller, "Mystical Literature," *Mysticism and Philosophical Analysis*, 96.

Critiques of Pluralism

The understanding of an indefinite pluralism of mystical forms has also come under serious attack. Anthony N. Perovich takes Katz to task for greatly overstating his conclusions. Two important points stand out in a recent article by him. First, Perovich, while agreeing to a weak thesis that some beliefs constitute some experiences, rejects the far more sweeping notion that all of our beliefs constitute all of our experiences. "Not every doctrine adhered to by an individual can plausibly be viewed as entering into the meanings of the terms he or she uses." Then an individual undergoing a mystical experience may have certain beliefs which do not define his or her experience. Another individual may have certain other extraneous beliefs that are not compatible with those of the first individual. But since neither of these two beliefs actually establishes the individuals' experiences, they may yet have common ground for their mystical lives. Perovich argues in response to Katz that "were he to claim that '*all* beliefs shape experience,' his thesis would be implausible, while if he were to claim that '*some* beliefs shape experience,' his thesis would become too weak to exclude shared mystical experience."[35]

Let us clarify this idea with an example. Let us say that a Christian holds two clusters of beliefs, A and B, where A determines his mystical experience, and B does not. A Hindu holds to belief clusters A and C, where C is inconsistent with B. But only A shapes his mystical experience, as it did for the Christian. Thus the Christian and the Hindu do not agree on many points, but can still have an identical experience because it is structured by A. For this argument to work, it is not necessary to show that this is an actual state of affairs. It suffices to note that it is a logical possibility. In that case we can say that it simply does not follow from the fact of distinct belief systems that there can be no common experiences.

---

[35]Anthony N. Perovich, Jr., "Mysticism and the Philosophy of Science," *Journal of Religion* 65 (1985): 68, 71.

Perovich's second attack on the Katz thesis also questions the assertion that our experiences are shaped universally by our beliefs. If that were so, it would have to be theoretically excluded that our experience could ever correct our beliefs. But the contrary is often true. We come into an experience with certain beliefs, but before we are through, we come out with our beliefs amended in order to suit the experience. Clearly there is a way in which our experiences can exceed the boundaries of our beliefs.[36] Thus Perovich has pointed out an essential asymmetry in the relationship between beliefs and experiences: Not all of our beliefs function in constituting each experience, and not all of our experiences are predetermined by our beliefs.

Similar reservations against the Katz thesis have been voiced by Deirdre Green, who asks us to distinguish the question of unity and diversity on four levels: "*(a)* ontological source of experience, *(b)* objective state, *(c)* total subjective experience, *(d)* interpretation." Green's point is that plurality on any three of these levels would still not preclude unity on a fourth. For example, "two different mystics could have different experiences of the same Absolute Reality." In addition, Green is not convinced that one has to stipulate absolute diversity in mystical experience. "Nevertheless, it remains true that within this diversity we are discerning unity which ties the different experiences together so that we are able to speak of each as an example of 'mysticism'; and it seems to me that Katz is in danger of losing sight of this."[37]

Assessing the Issue

Let us now attempt to adjudicate among the many positions described above. To do so, we can delineate some basic distinctions and commitments.

---

[36]Ibid., 73.
[37]Deirdre Green, "Unity in Diversity," *Scottish Journal of Religious Studies* 3 (1982): 53, 52.

The Integrity of the Individual's Experience

When Keller says that mystics would not normally claim to have experienced "mysticism,"[38] he must surely be right. As we have seen, Happold tries to make a case for mysticism in general, as though any tradition happens to be just a convenient way of achieving the larger goal of generic mystical experience. But Happold's position must be regarded as the atypical view of a modern scholar with a predisposition toward abstract generalizations. It is certainly not the view of the overwhelming majority of mystics themselves.

Consider, for example, the Christian mystics of the Middle Ages. They realized that there were possible mystical experiences other than their own. But they sought to distance themselves from them as far as possible. St. John of the Cross and Teresa of Ávila were always trying to guard themselves against potential counterfeits. And in a rather sophisticated treatment, Blessed John Ruysbroeck distinguished between different forms of mysticism.[39] In fact, he becomes the inspiration for Zaehner's classifications. How shocked these saints would be to find out that actually when they thought they experienced the love of Jesus, they merely experienced "mysticism" under one particular interpretation! Katz and his followers must be right in claiming that no Procrustean bed could be tighter than one that obliterates the distinctions between Vedantic monism and Jewish cabala mysticism as merely superficial and verbal only. The integrity of each tradition and its form of mysticism must be respected by the scholar.

And yet it also seems wrong to deny any commonality. Does one have to rule out all possibility of speaking of mysticism as a whole? Let us clarify what "common language" and "common experience" might mean. We are in a sense reversing the process of Katz's argumentation.

---

[38] Keller, "Mystical Literature," 96.
[39] John Ruysbroeck, *Spiritual Espousals*, 167ff., in Zaehner, *Mysticism: Sacred and Profane*, 172.

Family Resemblances and Essences

One of the points Katz makes is that one cannot draw inferences from similar language because, as he said, the meaning of language is derived from its context. A word used in a Hindu context is bound to have a different meaning if used in a Christian context. Thus even if a Hindu described an experience in a particular way, and a Christian uses identical words to describe a personal experience, we would not be entitled to infer that they were both referring to the same experience.

However, one might be inclined to view this analysis as overstated. If it were true in such absolute terms, it would be difficult to see how there could be any communication between Christian and Hindu. If we approach the Hindu's report from a Christian context, how can we have any idea at all as to what the Hindu has been saying? In fact, since all of us live within different contexts, one could even begin to wonder how we can communicate at all. If one ponders the barriers to shared meaning long enough, one can pretty easily convince oneself that no one can understand what anyone else is saying.

Such a conclusion would not just be overstated—it would be absurd. Presumably Katz would quickly point out that there are mechanisms at work within human communication that make for a shared world and, thereby, for shared language meaning. And now we can reply to such an escape that it is quite right, but then we may stipulate some such mechanisms among different mystical traditions as well.

Katz's point on language turns out to be a point of hermeneutics, the science of understanding and interpretation. Ever since Schleiermacher, Western thinkers have attempted to cope with the dilemma that one can understand a person only when one knows that person's context, but one cannot know his context unless one understands the person.[40]

---

[40]Friedrich Schleiermacher, *Hermeneutics: The Handwritten Manuscripts*, ed. Heinz Kimmerle, trans. James Duke and Jack Forstman (Missoula, Mont.: Scholars Press, 1977).

However, there has also been a traditional answer, based largely on common sense, that goes a long way toward solving that problem. One can concede that, on the one hand, the further the gap in life world between two individuals, the more difficult it is to understand each other. Yet, on the other hand, one may argue that there is enough shared context simply in being human that there is always the possibility for some rudimentary understanding.[41]

To respond to this sort of problem, Ludwig Wittgenstein suggested the model of family resemblance.[42] He began by denying that a word used in various contexts manifests an underlying essence, or that the meaning of a word comes from always referring to a particular object. But just because there is no permanent meaning for a word does not mean that a word used in two different contexts must have two different meanings. These two usages may share a family resemblance.

It is a rare family in which every member partakes of exactly the same features. More often than not, one can identify a pool of common features—the color of the hair, shape of the mouth, size of the nose, shade of the eyes, and so on—and every family member has some but not usually all of those features. We recognize the family resemblance, even without being able to point to any one essential characteristic.

A model such as this one can adequately respond to Katz's challenge.[43] We do not need to assume a constant invariable meaning for a term in order to retain a certain amount of shared meaning. When a Christian and a Hindu both assert that they have experienced union with the absolute, do they

[41]See my articles, "Philosophical Presuppositions Affecting Hermeneutics," in Hermeneutics, Inerrancy, and the Bible, ed. Earl D. Radmacher and Robert D. Preus (Grand Rapids: Zondervan, 1984), 495–513; and "Humility and Commitment: An Approach to Modern Hermeneutics," Themelios 11 (1986): 83–88.

[42]Ludwig Wittgenstein, Philosophical Investigations, trans. G. E. M. Anscombe, 3rd ed. (New York: Macmillan, 1958), 32, sec. 67.

[43]Another possibility would be a Thomistic approach: analogia duorum ad tertium (the analogy of two to a third). I would be even more sympathetic to such an approach. But since it involves greater metaphysical assumptions, it would not be as handy an answer to Katz, who is certainly not a Thomist.

both mean exactly the same thing? Certainly not, but we may say that their words have similar meaning because they share family resemblance. We cannot theoretically rule out the possibility that they both mean totally different things, but such a situation would be highly remarkable. In light of all of the clues suggesting that their experiences can be similar, it makes sense to assume that their language is not entirely dissimilar either.

We need to support the claim that their experiences can be similar, but before taking up that issue, we need to clarify the fact that we are far from being done with the problem of mystical language. The problem discussed here is a "horizontal" one—whether two mystics may mean similar things with similar words. But the larger problem is a "vertical" one—whether language used with reference to mysticism has any meaning at all. What two mystics express with their words may be common gibberish, but nothing more. We shall devote an entire chapter to this question below. But first we return to the present thread of argument: can we speak meaningfully of shared experience?

Similar Experiences

If we can show that there is a possibility of common or similar experience, then we may expect resemblance in word meaning and may allow that mysticism represents, if not a *perennial philosophy*, at least not a hopelessly disparate pluralism either. But does it make sense to allow for a notion of similar experience?

Again, integrity demands that we rule out, on the basis of the evidence, the idea that our representative Hindu and Christian have the same or identical experience. But we can make a case that, just as there can be family resemblance in language, there can be family resemblance in experience.

In one sense, an experience is always private. This is the case if we construe an experience as immediate awareness. No one else feels it when a pin pricks my finger, when I have a headache, and when I am excited about a surprise I have planned. Furthermore, two people in one situation may give radically different reports of what they have experienced. Everyone knows of the discrepancies in testimony that witnesses to the same event may give. Or perhaps one has heard a person react to a book, a movie, or a sermon, and it sounds like something totally different from one's own impression of the same thing. Such cases make Katz's point for him that one's preconceptions define one's experience.

But let us consider the case of a man's describing a movie he saw on television. His reaction to it is very different from a friend's. He emphasizes different aspects of the movie, evaluates the characters and plot differently, and has a different summary of it. Perhaps he even misrepresents some of the facts of the movie, as far as his friend can tell. Now it is possible to push this example to the limit where the two friends never realize that they have both seen the same movie. But we are not forced to that conclusion, even if the two descriptions are radically different. For underlying their different points of view is the ontological reality of the movie. And sooner or later enough clues will accumulate to enable the friends to decide that they have both seen the same movie.

The beliefs someone uses to describe an experience may be the beliefs that one uses to constitute the experience, but they may also be a subsequent interpretation of the experience. Consider the following example: Person A says, "I have just seen *Gone with the Wind*. It is an exciting historical romance." Person B says, "I have just seen *Gone with the Wind*. It is a long and tedious Civil War soap opera." By a strict application of Katz's criterion, one would have to question whether both people saw the same movie. One might even wind up saying that the fact that both people placed their experience under the heading "Gone with the Wind" is purely a coincidence from which we may not draw any conclusions. But that approach would eliminate all common experience and possibly lead to solipsism.

To sum up this argument:

1. We must beware of inferring similarity, let alone identity, of experience too hastily.
2. But we cannot a priori rule out all similarity of the experience either, even if it is described differently.
3. We can tell if a similar experience is behind divergent descriptions on the basis of testimonies. If there are enough references to something similar in two accounts, we can postulate a core experience. This analysis would come without guarantees of certainty.

We quoted Katz above with the assertion "in so far as words mean anything," one cannot "equate the experience of *nirvana* and *devekuth* on the basis of evidence."[44] This point can stand. But we can also say that insofar as the testimony of mystics has any meaning, we cannot rule out all similarities. William James and Stace, for example, did not come up with their lists of characteristics of mystical experience, even if they include some arbitrary judgments, without sifting through much testimony from mystics themselves.

A Modest Conclusion

The present discussion can be interpreted as very typical of trends of the twentieth century. Not too long ago it was fashionable to search for the kernel of truth behind the multiplicity of all religious tradition, including mysticism. That agenda lent itself to the propounding of a perennial philosophy that supposedly manifests itself in all of the many mystical phenomena. The heavy-handedness of this approach was bound to lead to a countermovement asserting the uniqueness of each tradition without a shared core. In between these two approaches one finds a number of thinkers who defend unity within a diversity of types, an approach that often seems to be motivated by apologetic purposes, distinguishing "true" mysticism from the rest of mysticism.

But as I have tried to show in the last section, much of

---

[44]Katz, "Language, Epistemology, and Mysticism," 39.

this discussion has been nurtured by overstatement. The person who approaches this subject without an ax to grind should have little problem coming to the question of unity and diversity in mysticism on a similar basis as other concepts, such as worship, prayer, bliss, and so forth. Let us conclude this topic by drawing a parallel to the concept of worship.

First, worship cuts across many traditions. Many, if not most, religions have a practice of worship. Sometimes it is more easily recognized than others. There is even a secular concept of worship, such as when we say of someone that he or she worships money. This diversity resembles the diversity of mystical traditions.

Second, there is no single underlying concept of worship. The attempt to identify a core notion of worship will either fail or result in a tradition-biased distinction between real worship and not-so-real worship, with shades of legitimacy in between. For the same reason we reject the idea of a perennial philosophy.

Third, each tradition of worship is unique and deserves to be studied within its own context and meaning. The best way to understand the Hindu worship of Rama is not by drawing comparisons to the Christian's worship of Jesus but by letting Hindus speak for themselves about their intentions and conceptions. Similarly, a fair understanding of a mystical tradition needs to come to terms with it on its own ground.

Fourth, we can discern patterns of similarity when comparing traditions of worship. Some traditions worship many gods, others just one god. In some traditions worship is a personal ritual, in others it is a spontaneous group activity. There are traditions that see worship as the highest religious activity, while in others it is considered inferior to practical deeds. In short, we can, without making judgments on truth or reality, come up with classifications of types of worship. These are not necessarily "real" in the sense that reality itself delimits the types, but they can be legitimate combinations of traditions that share a point in common and that exclude some other point. In the same vein, it is legitimate to discern various types of mysticism as convenient attempts at classification. Zaehner's three types would be a good case in point, though we must beware of seeing his types as absolute with no possibility of overlap or as inherently indicative of truth judgments.

Finally, without being able to identify the essence of all worship, it still makes sense to speak of the practice of worship, the concept of worship, or the general phenomenon of worship. One could write an informed and fair book on worship in the world's religions without ever having to compromise oneself into a univocal obligatory definition of worship.

Our parallel is this: Resisting the imperialism of the perennial philosophy does not entail having to abandon all talk of mysticism in general. After all of the distinctions have been observed and duly registered, it is still possible to think of mysticism as a general phenomenon, so long as one does not legislate what the core or essence of this phenomenon must be, or obliterate the uniqueness of each mystical tradition. Thus it is also legitimate to defend a tentative general definition, such as the one proposed above: the unmediated link to the absolute. Then the key to remaining honest in one's endeavor is to see traditions that do not fit the definition not as exceptions to true mysticism but as legitimate forms of mysticism not accommodated by our definition.

Thus we find ourselves at the end of this chapter with two important clues to take on our quest. First, we may continue to speak of "mysticism in general," so long as we do not read too much into that phrase. Second, any answer to questions of final truth cannot come from mysticism in general but from engaging a specific tradition with its unique claim.

4

Does Mysticism Have an Objective Referent?

WE HAVE DEFINED MYSTICISM IN TERMS OF A PER-
sonal unmediated link to an absolute. Furthermore, we have
allowed that it is permissible to speak of it as a general
phenomenon without doing violence to the integrity of
particular traditions. Does that mean that there really is an
absolute with which people link up? Must there not be an
objective reality behind the experiences either as its cause or
as its effect?

This question can be understood in two different ways. It
can be seen as asking either whether there is one particular
absolute behind all of the various experiences, or whether all
of the different experiences must include some sort of
transcendent or absolute object, no matter of what description. We shall focus on the second, more modest, understanding of the question. Nevertheless, we shall see that some
writers have confused an affirmative answer to the second
version with an affirmative answer to the first. But that
obviously does not follow. Even if it is true that everyone
experiences some transcendent reality, it does not follow that
they experience the same transcendent reality. Stace has
provided an argument proceeding from the second to the first
version, but only by positing the category "transsubjective."[1]

---

[1] Stace, *Mysticism and Philosophy*, 161–78.

We will discuss this point below. Before going any further, though, we need to address an important preliminary question.

From Experience to the Transcendent

It could be the case that this entire chapter is an exercise in futility. We are concerned with finding an answer to the question of whether the mystic's experience gives us cause to postulate an objective referent for the experience. But this question may be in principle unanswerable. It could be (and has been) argued that it is intrinsically impossible to arrive at any nonempirical conclusions from empirically based premises. The deduction of an objective referent from a mystical experience would then only be one case in point. Alfred North Whitehead stated the basic principle this way: "Any proof which commences with the considerations of the character of the actual world cannot rise above the actuality of the world. It can only discover all the features in the world as experienced."[2] Thus if we begin with experience, we will end up with an analysis of experience, nothing more.

But Thomas Aquinas has provided a very telling reply to this kind of argument in the course of his discussion on the existence of God.[3] He concedes the point made by Whitehead and many others before him. Simply accumulating data of experience does not allow us to transcend experience. But we can confine ourselves to experience and test our data to see whether they do not bear the marks of something transcendent to experience. Though we may not be able to see God by looking at the world, we may be able to see the effects of God in the world.

Aquinas's "five ways" proceed by analyzing five different experienced aspects of the world, and in each case they conclude that these things could not be if there was no God

---

[2]Alfred North Whitehead, *Religion in the Making* (New York: World, 1960), 69.

[3]Thomas Aquinas, *Summa Theologica* 1.2.2.

causing them. A similar methodological understanding can also legitimate our question concerning an objective referent for mystical experience. We are not trying to find the absolute in the experience, but we are looking at the experience to see whether it bears the marks of the absolute. Are there aspects to the experience that can be explained only by positing a real absolute that causes them? This question cannot be dismissed out of hand except by maintaining an initial prejudice against the possibility of an absolute. Such an objection, though, would have to be rejected or supported on other grounds; it would not render the question itself illegitimate. Thus the question is: do the various mystical experiences give evidence of an absolute beyond the experience?

The Argument from Unanimity

The strongest case of this sort has been made by advocates of the so-called argument from unanimity. Given our conclusion in the preceding chapter, it is evident that we cannot endorse such an argument. There is no mystical unanimity. But it does no harm to present the argument, for it opens up further lines of argumentation.

A popular version of the argument from unanimity comes from the pen of C. D. Broad.[4] Broad's argument is most forceful because of his care and understatement in argumentation. We can summarize it in the following way:

1. Mystical experience occurs within backgrounds that are highly diverse in time, place, tradition, and interpretation.
2. Nevertheless there are (probably) certain common characteristics within all of the diversity.
3. These common characteristics distinguish mystical experience from all other experience.
4. Therefore there is the likelihood that in mystical

[4]C. D. Broad, *Religion, Philosophy, and Psychical Research* (London: Routledge and Kegan Paul, 1953), 172–97.

experience persons come into contact with a different form of reality than they meet in other experience.

This argument manifests an evident strength as well as an evident weakness. The strength centers on the first premise. We can classify this argument as an example of J. S. Mill's method of agreement. As an inductive argument, it tries to establish the probable cause of a phenomenon in a variety of different situations. Of all of the diverse components of each of the situations, it points to the one factor common to them all as causing the phenomenon in question.

Let us assume that we have four different situations: *A*, *B*, *C*, and *D*. They have the following characteristics:

A: 1, 2, 3, 4
B: 1, 5, 6, 7
C: 1, 8, 9, 10
D: 1, 11, 12, 13

Now if, despite all of the diversity, within these situations there arises a common phenomenon, say 14, it may be valid to infer that this phenomenon was caused by factor 1.[5] Clearly this kind of argument is strongest when the diversity of the sample situations is greatest. And here we have the point of greatest strength in Broad's argument.

But the point of greatest weakness is not too far removed. Let us assume this fantastic diversity in mystical situations. Let us also, only for the sake of argument, grant that there is some kind of common core to all of the various experiences. It still would not follow that there was some sort of an objective reality causing these experiences. Somehow there must be a reason to make a causal inference to begin with. If there is none in any one given instance, then there is no justification for attributing one in a multiplicity of instances.

---

[5]The inference will be more or less probable, depending on the specific situation. For example, only by examining the specific situation could we say whether factor 1 caused factor 14 or vice versa, or whether a causal relationship is plausible at all.

Specifically, we are here attacking the notion that the experience must be caused by a reality beyond the subjective faculties of the individual having the experience. Of course it would be very hard (if not impossible) to maintain the idea of a purely uncaused experience. But it is legitimate to divide experiences into those with an objective external cause and those with an internal cause. An example of the former would be the pleasure of eating a five-scoop chocolate fudge ice cream cone. An example of the latter might be the simple contemplation of such an indulgence. Thinking of this cone evokes images and makes a chocolate lover feel pleasurable even though he or she may never have eaten one and will never indulge in such a monstrosity. It is not necessary that there be such a cone for one to have an experience involving it as an image or a concept. Thus it is sometimes necessary, if one wants to draw an external causal inference, to show why this should be done, namely why one should make an external connection to begin with.

Broad does exactly that. He develops a principle for going beyond the experience to an external cause.

> Where there is a nucleus of agreement between the experiences of men in different places, times, and traditions, and when they all tend to put much the same kind of interpretation on the cognitive content of the experiences, it is reasonable to ascribe this agreement to their all being in contact with a certain aspect of reality *unless* there be some positive reason to think otherwise.[6]

There is a lot to be said on behalf of this principle. Its essence is that, as human beings, we usually assume that what we say to each other is true, unless we have good reason to doubt someone's word. It is not unreasonable to think that this principle is implicit in any attempt to have a human community. A simple application of this principle to our topic would then be to consult the mystic and take his or her word for the issue at hand.

[6]Broad, *Religion, Philosophy, and Psychical Research*, 197.

But as we saw in the previous chapter, writers such as Broad violate their own principle. For it is highly questionable that there is a "nucleus of agreement" among the experiences of the mystics, and it is just plain false that "they all tend to put much the same kind of interpretation on the cognitive content" of their experiences. The Christian mystic believes that his experience is caused by God, the Hindu by Brahman, and so forth. To stipulate a common generic "objective aspect of reality" behind these experiences requires an assumption that goes directly counter to what the mystics themselves are saying. That Broad does not himself believe his principle is made clear when earlier he issues the disclaimer, "But I do not think that there is any reason to suppose that this reality is personal."[7]

But let us assume, again purely for the sake of argument, that there is in fact unanimity among the mystics. Let us say that they all report that they had a similar experience that was caused by some factor R. The argument that R is real would still not be very plausible because there is good reason to "think otherwise." The reason is that the rest of humanity has never experienced R in this way. The argument from unanimity is not an argument based on a unanimous consensus of all human beings, but at best the unanimous consensus of a small group of experts. William James argues,

> The utmost they can ever ask of us in this life is to admit that they have established a presumption. They form a consensus and have an unequivocal outcome; and it would be odd, mystics might say, if such a unanimous type of experience should prove altogether wrong. At bottom, however, this would only be an appeal to numbers, like the appeal of rationalism the other way; and the appeal to numbers has no logical force. If we acknowledge it, it is for "suggestive," not for logical reasons: we follow the majority because to do [so] suits our life.[8]

---

[7]Ibid., 173.
[8]James, *Varieties*, 332–33.

Marvin Kohl comments that James "takes a favourite defense of mysticism and turns it back on its users." He goes on: "If the mystic is under no obligation to be restricted to the majority of mankind, then surely the rest of mankind is under no obligation to follow the mystic. If the appeal is solely to experience, then one cannot demand that people believe something which they do not or cannot experience."[9]

Thus the so-called argument from unanimity fails on two counts: First, there simply is not the kind of unanimity that the argument is predicated on. Second, even if there were as much unanimous consensus as the advocates of the argument claim, it would still not be sufficient to establish what they hope to prove. Of course, saying that the argument fails is to assert nothing more than just that. It does not mean that there is no objective reality behind any or all mystical experience; it simply means that this argument has not shown such to be the case.

Subjective or Objective?

If the argument from unanimity had worked, it would have provided a shortcut toward establishing the truth claims made by any one mystic. If the Sufi, for example, claims to have experienced Allah, Broad's argument would have allowed us to respond by saying, "Well, we don't know if it is Allah that you have experienced, but we can grant that you have at least come into contact with the kind of ill-defined reality that is usually encountered by mystics." It is doubtful that the Sufi would be any more satisfied with that answer than a skeptic would be. Fortunately they are both safe, since the argument intended to provide such a license apparently does not work.

But what of the Sufi's claim? Or what of the claims made by Sankara, St. John of the Cross, or Black Elk, for that matter? Each of them believed to have been in touch with, not some generic reality, but a very specific reality. Must we take their

---

[9]Kohl, "Unanimity Argument," 272.

word for it that there is such a reality and that they have encountered it? To what extent is their experience subjective or objective?

Subjectivity

It is clear that mystical experience is subjective. But there are different ways in which we can use the word "subjective," and we need to be careful lest we equivocate on its meaning and draw erroneous conclusions. The obvious given use of the term "subjective" for mystical experience is that it is private. The unmediated link to the absolute is limited to the individual's life world and interpretive framework. No mystics ever explain their experience from outside of their personal background.

A second use of the term "subjective" centers on the type of truth claim made by the individual. The mystical experience is supposed to be one of direct awareness. This fact would align the mystical experience with other examples of direct awareness, such as feeling pain or seeing red. The instances are similar in that the experience itself brings with it a certain indubitability. How can anyone doubt whether I feel pain or see red? I cannot doubt that I am having these experiences myself, and though someone may question whatever objective reality I posit behind my experiences, everyone will have to take my word for the claim that I am having them (even if it means raising questions on my sanity). Now mystics claim to have had a direct awareness of something absolute. And their reports entail that same kind of immediately given certainty. No matter how we feel about their ontological claims, they believe that they have been in direct touch with something absolute, and for them that settles the issue.

But there is a third meaning to "subjective" that we can apply to mystics' experiences only at pain of directly contradicting them. This meaning denies any reality to the experience outside of the mystics' own subjectivity. Under this meaning there would simply be nothing more to the experience than the experience. Even though the mystics may claim to have been in touch with some reality other than themselves, that claim would then be a mistake on their part. Frequently in this use of the term, a mystic experience is identified with an emotion or a feeling whose objective reality begins and ends with the individual.

However, if this third use of the term is appropriate, then we are no longer doing justice to the mystic's own description. Of course a member of a different tradition will want to do exactly that. A Christian, for example, will dispute that the Hindu really has experienced Brahman, and the Sufi may question whether the Christian has had direct contact with Jesus. In any event, it is certainly a mistake to label the mystical experience as nothing more than emotions,[10] for, as William James has pointed out,[11] it usually carries with it a "noetic quality," namely, the mystic believes that he or she has acquired some kind of knowledge. Strong feelings and emotions may accompany the experience, but it would have to be severely truncated to reduce the experience to emotion alone.

Now the knowledge component may lack the objective reference claimed for it, and so it may still be subjective, but that case would still not be the same thing as reducing it all to emotion. Let us now examine the kind of objectivity claimed for the experience by many mystics.

Objectivity

As soon as we start to talk about objectivity in the mystical experience, the issue gets extremely cloudy because mystics themselves are not happy with the term. We can see a wide variety of interpretations across the traditions.

Let us be clear what is at stake here. Certainly the issue is

[10]See Stace, *Mysticism and Philosophy*, 14–17.
[11]James, *Varieties*, 300.

not whether the mystic does objectively have his or her experience. We can divide this issue into two parts. First, for those mystics who deny objective reference, what do they mean? Second, for those mystics who claim objective reference, what is the warrant for their claim?

The first of these two questions may not be rationally answerable. If the mystical experience is neither purely subjective nor objective, then what is it? Many mystics seem to have placed themselves into exactly this position of denying both subjectivity and objectivity. Consider the Vedantic mystic, who believes that atman (his true self) is identical with Brahman (the universal absolute). If such a mystic was to say that this realization is purely subjective, we would surely deny the existence status being claimed for Brahman. On the other hand, it does not make sense to call it objective either, since at the heart of it is something that is true within the person and not external. Atman-Brahman is supposed to transcend the categories of objectivity. It is neither one nor a combination of the two.

In order to solve the dilemma, W. T. Stace has come up with the category "transsubjectivity."[12] This word expresses the idea that the mystical experience is not merely subjective in that it goes beyond the person's subjectivity. Furthermore, since according to Stace's thesis there is a universal core to mystical experience, the term also indicates the reference point beyond the experience of all the individual selves to a "universal self." Thus, even though Stace does not want to admit objectivity, he tries to raise the experience beyond subjectivity to transsubjectivity.

Stace's thesis has been criticized frequently and, I would say, adequately. William Wainwright, for example, has argued that Stace has not been successful in making his case. He states that "it seems fair to say that if the experience really has no object, it is not even a candidate for a cognitive experience." Furthermore, "the most that Stace's argument

---

[12]Stace, *Mysticism and Philosophy*, 146–52.

does is to show that the mystical experience is neither objective nor subjective in [his] explained sense."[13]

We can add to such observations the point that Stace's idea shows up the mistake of abstracting the experience too much from its interpretive framework. The notion of trans-subjectivity is tenable only on the assumption that we can pare away from all mystical experiences all of the characteristics that keep them from being "pure," including the conceptual systems in which they occur. And of course, aside from the objections raised against that methodology in the last chapter, we already began this study by pointing out in chapter 2 the need to examine mysticism as occurring in conceptual and religious schemes, not purely as an isolated experience. But when we do, the fact that transsubjectivity is inadequate seems inevitable. In Wainwright's words, "Although mystics sometimes speak as if the duality of subject and object were overcome, so that the experience and that which is experienced become identical, it is also clear that they frequently speak as if the experience had an object which is not identical with the mystic or his experience."[14]

This statement is true even of a Vedantist who refers to Brahman. One could even go so far as to say that the incessant protests against objectivity demonstrate the inevitability of making an inference of objectivity.

But that observation brings us to the second question. What is the warrant for ascribing objectivity to the mystic's reference point, particularly to the reality of the absolute? The answer can be separated into two parts—for the mystic and for the outsider. To the former, there can be no question of any verification beyond the experience itself. We have already aligned it with other forms of direct awareness such as seeing a color or feeling pain. To have this kind of awareness is sufficient proof that the object of awareness exists. Similar things must be true for the mystic's understanding of the

---

[13]William J. Wainwright, "Stace and Mysticism," *Journal of Religion* 50 (1970): 141, 143.
[14]Ibid., 143.

absolute. For the mystic there can be no questioning of it, since he or she has experienced it directly. As Alan Watts states, "As ultimate and infinite Reality there is no external standpoint from which to doubt it or prove it. We are compelled, then, to take it as given."[15]

Of course that compulsion does not prove that the absolute is real, but only that the mystic cannot deny the reality based on personal experience.

But who is compelled to accept it as given? The mystic who had a particular experience is compelled, but no one else. The epistemology of immediacy guarantees absolute certainty to the one who has had a certain direct awareness; everyone else will simply have to take that one's word for it. This stricture even applies among mystics. Mystic A cannot test mystic B's experience, and so forth. Thus there is simply no access to the mystic's object of experience for an outsider seeking some reason to accept the mystic's report as true.

A mystic of Watts's persuasion may exult in this epistemology of immediacy, but for the rest of us it becomes intolerable, if we are trying to pursue truth. After all, mystics claim to have had immediate awareness of Brahman, Jesus, Allah, the Six Grandfathers, and so forth. Unless one wants to subscribe to the most irrational pantheon of absolutes, some of them mutually exclusive—a position that Stace and others seem implicitly to be taking—one has to decide between claims. Perhaps none is true, but they certainly cannot all be true.

Thus we return again to the earlier point. In analyzing mysticism, we cannot limit ourselves to the experience; we need to look at the whole frame of reference for each given experience. The question of truth cannot be settled within the experience, but only if we test the scheme in which the

---

[15]Alan Watts, *The Supreme Identity: An Essay in Oriental Metaphysic and the Christian Religion* (New York: Random House, 1972), 49. Cf. also Robert Oakes, "Religious Experience and Epistemological Miracles: A Moderate Defense of Theistic Mysticism," *International Journal for Philosophy of Religion* 12 (1981): 97–110.

experience fits and of which the experience may be only a small part. For example, if a Christian mystic claims a mystical experience with God, the experience itself cannot convince others of the reality of God. That fact would have to be demonstrated some other way, perhaps by means of one of the classic arguments.

Such an assessment means, then, that questions of truth and objectivity need to be dealt with in the traditional manner for issues of religion—on the basis of evidence, argumentation, apologetics, or whatever comes to hand. But the mystical experience itself can have no epistemological effect. It should be clear here that this conclusion does not mean that it is impossible to settle the question of truth and objectivity, let alone that all experiences are equal. But this question needs to be approached on independent grounds. Thus, as a Christian, it is for other reasons than the nature of the experience itself that I reject the objective reference of, say, a Hindu's mystical experience. I reject Hinduism as a religion; hence I reject the experience contained therein. The above argument shows that it is legitimate to take this approach.

A Natural Faculty

After the previous section, it suddenly becomes easy to claim that a mystical experience does not guarantee any reality. But having refuted the arguments from a mystical experience to a reality, we need to give some sort of account of why so many people in so many different traditions think they experience a reality. The problem comes in two parts. First, we need to show how it is possible that many people from many different times and traditions have such remarkably similar experiences. After all, in refuting the supposed unanimity, we must not forget that we did not deny similarity. We resorted to the idea of family resemblance earlier. Now that we are no longer burdened with identity or unanimity, we can even go so far as to say that there is a lot of similarity spanning the centuries and belief systems. How can we account for this similarity if we do not concede an underlying objective reality? Second, we need to show how someone within a belief system that we might deem false can have an experience of direct awareness of realities claimed by that belief system. For example, if Hinduism is not a true religion, how is it possible that someone could have a Hindu mystical experience?

An easy answer, of course, would be to return to an interpretation of mysticism as pure subjectivity. If we deny that any mystical experience has any objective reference, then our problem is solved. But as we said earlier, that position would also overstate the boundary of proper inference from the facts. Furthermore, this study is premised on a particular belief system, namely evangelical Christianity, and we ought not at this point deny the possibility of a Christian mystical experience with God in Jesus Christ. Thus it would be counterproductive to deny all possibility of objectivity. A Muslim might want to take the same attitude to advance a special pleading for Islam.

Thus we need a model that both allows for objectivity where warranted and retains subjectivity alone where warranted (where what is warranted in each case is determined on extraneous grounds). Such a model is available to us in the form of a theory of a natural mystical faculty. We may posit a natural human capacity for mystical experience that can be activated either purely subjectively or by objective causes. By way of analogy, we could refer to human emotional capacities—for example, the potential to feel happy. A person can feel happy for all sorts of reasons: imaginary, subjective, fictitious, objective, external, religious, and so on. We cannot infer, simply from someone's being happy, the cause of the happiness, but we can pass judgment on the realities that the person alleges to be behind the happiness.

Maybe something similar can be true for mysticism. We can posit as a basic trait of the human mind that it can undergo a mystical experience brought on by all sorts of causes, both internal and external. It could be triggered by physical activation, including drugs or other physiological stimuli. It could also occur purely self-induced within false belief systems. Finally, one could say that it can also be part of the experience of linking up with a genuine reality, as a Christian might claim for God.

Such a general thesis of a mystical capacity was implicit in the teachings of Blessed John Ruysbroeck in the Middle Ages. Ruysbroeck considered the fact that there were monistic mystics, those whose experience did not center on God, who were not a threat to his Christian beliefs and experience. Nor did he deny the monist the reality of his or her experience. Ruysbroeck simply saw the monistic experience as a natural human act of self-transcending that has all of the marks of encountering a deeper reality but that in the end comes up empty.[16]

Fascinating support for this theory has been claimed within the context of physiological psychology. Arthur J. Deikman believes that he has isolated two different modes of consciousness in the human being. The active or objective mode of consciousness is the way of organizing knowledge, manipulating the environment, and bringing about physical results for the individual (e.g. biological survival). The passive or perceptive mode, on the other hand, is a more passive intake of the environment. The active mode emphasizes the distinction between the individual and his or her environment. The passive mode tends toward unity of the individual with the environment and a gradual submerging of one's identity. We can contrast these two modes as shown on the following page:[17]

---

[16]Ruysbroeck, *Spiritual Espousals*, 167, cited in Zaehner, *Mysticism: Sacred and Profane*, 173.

[17]Arthur J. Deikman, *The Observing Self: Mysticism and Psychotherapy* (Boston: Beacon Press, 1982), 72. See also Stanley A. Nevins, "Mystical Consciousness and the Problem of Personal Identity," *Philosophy Today* 20 (1976): 149–56.

Active/Objective Mode	Passive/Perceptive Mode
manipulation of environment	intake of environment
striate muscle system dominant	sensory-perceptual system dominant
sympathetic nervous system most prominent	parasympathetic system most prominent
baseline tension increased	baseline tension decreased
focal attention	diffuse attention
object-based logic	paralogical thought processes
heightened boundary perception	decreased boundary perception
dominance of formal character over sensory	dominance of sensory over formal
shape and meaning over color and texture	color and texture over shape and meaning
nurtured in the maturation process	typical in infancy

What Deikman shows us is that apparently the human organism comes equipped with all of the necessary prerequisites for a mystical experience. All that is needed is that for some reason the perceptive mode is emphasized or isolated, and an experience that has all of the characteristics of mysticism results.

Some writers have taken Deikman's conclusions as their cue for endorsing a purely naturalistic, even exclusively physical, basis for mystical experience.[18] But that would be going too far, for two reasons. First, Deikman's conclusions do not prove a physical theory any more than any other psychologist can experimentally verify materialism. The fact that mental events may be accompanied by physical events does not prove the identity of mental and physical events. Such an identity is only a philosophical presumption. Second, to show that there is such a natural function in human beings does not preclude the possibility that it can be activated by supernatural causes. If Deikman has succeeded in showing that there is

[18]E.g. Norman Melchert, "Mystical Experience and Ontological Claims," *Philosophy and Phenomenological Research* 37 (1977): 445–63.

a natural mystical capacity, then he has still not shown that this is all there is to mysticism.

But what Deikman has demonstrated is a way of being able to show simultaneously why some mystical experiences (i.e. those that are nothing more than pure receptive consciousness) lack objective content, whereas apparently others (those in which the perceptive consciousness is open to God) can refer to ontological realities.

Thus we can conclude this section with the hypothesis that each person has a natural mystical faculty that may be activated naturally or by God. Just as we have a natural capacity to love or have faith, which may also be directly stimulated by God but often is not, so it is possible that our mystical awareness can be stimulated by God but often is not.

The results of this chapter, then are twofold. First, we reasoned that no argument based on the mystical experience can show that there is an ontological reality behind the experience. But second, we have argued that we cannot preclude a reality behind the experience either. Which mystic has the reality? To answer this question, we need to evaluate the various belief systems. This question cannot be settled on the basis of which mystic has the most impressive experience.

My personal commitment is to the truth of Christianity, a belief system based on many rational (and probably also some nonrational) grounds. Given that commitment, our reasoning now must be from the truth of the belief system to an evaluation of mysticism in its context.

Appendix

In *Philosophy of Religion*, Norman Geisler and I defend an argument for the reality of the Transcendent that looks suspiciously like the argument from unanimity that I rejected above.[19] According to this argument, there is a universal

---

[19]Norman L. Geisler and Winfried Corduan, *Philosophy of Religion*, 2nd ed. (Grand Rapids: Baker, 1988), 62–76.

experience of a need for the Transcendent, which can be explained only on the basis of the reality of the Transcendent. This argument, however, differs from the so-called argument from unanimity in several crucial ways.

First, the argument for the Transcendent is premised on a genuinely universal human experience. The argument does not restrict itself to the reports of a relatively exclusive number of individuals who are considered a part of that group first because they all say similar things. Rather, the argument for the Transcendent begins with the fact that all human beings demonstrate a need for transcendence, including those who deny the possibility of that need ever being met. If that statement is falsified, the argument would need to be rejected.

Second, the argument for the Transcendent includes many different ways in which human beings have demonstrated the need for the Transcendent. Mystical experience is only one member of the set of all of the transcendence-oriented experiences.

Third, the argument for the Transcendent is based on a demonstrated need and reasons that where there is a genuine need (as opposed to a wish or desire), there must be a real way of fulfilling it. Thus this argument manifests the causal link that is absent in the so-called argument from unanimity in mysticism. The mystical argument jumps from the experience to a reality behind the experience without legitimate warrant. But if a universal human need can be demonstrated, then there is motivation to posit a reality to meet that need.

The point here is not primarily to show why the argument for the Transcendent is successful whereas the mystic's argument from unanimity is not. More important, we are demonstrating rational reasons for believing one argument to be sound and for rejecting another. If it could be shown for mysticism alone that it (1) enjoys true human universality, (2) can accommodate all variations of experience coherently, and (3) leads us to posit a causal reality behind the experience, then the mystical argument from unanimity would also be acceptable.

5

Can Language Describe
Mystical Experience?

BEFORE ASKING HOW MYSTICISM FITS INTO A SPECIFI-
cally Christian framework, we need to clear up one further
philosophical obstacle: the problem of the appropriateness of
using language to express mystical ideas or to describe the
mystical experience. It might be questioned why we want to
tackle the question of language now, after concerning ourselves with the issues of definition, commonality, and ontological ground. Should not the question of language have been
settled in advance of those topics? It would indeed have been
reasonable to begin with the problem of language. On the
other hand, the problem of language could not have been
addressed properly without reference to the matters of common core and ontological reference. Hence, it seems best to
have left it to this point.

The Mystic's Paradox

As we saw earlier, William James made ineffability the
first characteristic of mystical experience.[1] W. T. Stace
includes it also, but only as the last category, and then with
some reservations.[2] In fact, it is next to impossible to read on

[1]James, *Varieties*, 299–300.
[2]Stace, *Mysticism and Philosophy*, 132.

the subject of mysticism without running into reference to ineffability. There does seem to be something of a consensus that it is not possible to do justice to a mystical experience with words. But why that should be so, and to what extent this ineffability constitutes a real limitation are questions on which the writers disagree. Leaving aside the former question of causes for the moment, let us first consider the problems ineffability may cause.

William Alston has given the problem a most acute formulation. In an article that has become something of a classic, Alston attacked the unqualified manner in which many writers have bandied about ineffability statements.[3] Consider the proposition "God is ineffable."[4] In a straightforward understanding of this sentence (i.e. without redefining words), it is highly problematic. Two basic criticisms are possible, according to Alston.

First, if God is ineffable, then no property can be predicated of him. This is the meaning given to the phrase by mystics themselves.[5] But simply by saying such a thing, the mystic is in fact predicating the property "ineffability" of God. This attack may seem overly simplistic, since the concept of ineffability is not supposed to say anything directly of God, but only to deny that anything can be said of God. Nonetheless, the mystic in making this statement is in some way asserting that this phenomenon of ineffability is appropriately asserted of God; something, no matter how negative or empty, is being said of God. But then, by saying that nothing can be said, the mystic is caught in a vicious circle. In Alston's words, "Aren't we in the position of being able to make a true statement only by doing the very things which the statement declares impossible, thereby falsifying it?"[6]

---

[3]William P. Alston, "Ineffability," *Philosophical Review* 65 (1956): 506–22.

[4]Ultimately, the same line of argumentation would also apply for other properties, such as "absolute," since they too are supposedly beyond our cognition.

[5]E.g. W. T. Stace, *Time and Eternity*, 33; cited in Alston, "Ineffability," 507.

[6]Alston, "Ineffability," 509.

Second, even assuming that we are not caught in this vicious circle, we are still in trouble by saying, "God is ineffable." For we are asserting ineffability of someone or something. In other words, we are not just saying, "There is ineffability," but we are ascribing this phenomenon to God (or whatever object of ineffability the mystic subscribes to). Thus we must have some sort of prior positive knowledge of God in order to say of him that he is ineffable. But then, once again the statement of his utter ineffability cannot be. Theoretically, someone could respond to this critique by saying that nothing more is meant by "God" than that to which we ascribe ineffability. But Alston rightly considers such a response to be fraudulent, for it is obvious that mystics do think of God as more than that, namely, as the absolute, the object of their experience, the supreme being in the universe, or similar things.

Thus Alston argues against unqualified assertions of divine ineffability by mystics. Whenever they say that God is ineffable, they are in fact contradicting themselves. Samuel Johnson stated the matter succinctly with reference to Jacob Boehme, "If Jacob saw the unutterable, Jacob should not have tried to utter it."[7]

Reasons for Ineffability

Conventional wisdom holds that before one can solve any problem, one needs to isolate the reason or cause for the problem. If conventional wisdom is correct on this point, then the problem of mystical ineffability may never be solved. J. Kellenberger has indicated some, but only some, of the variety of alleged causes with which we need to contend here. He shows first of all that mystics are not agreed as to what it is that is supposed to be ineffable. The object of ineffability

---

[7]Cited in Alasdair MacIntyre, "Is Religious Language So Idiosyncratic That We Can Hope for No Account of It?" in *Religious Language and the Problem of Religious Knowledge,* ed. Ronald E. Santoni (Bloomington: Indiana University Press, 1968), 50.

could be (1) the absolute, (2) the truth (or knowledge), (3) the self, (4) the experience, or (5) any combination thereof.[8] Furthermore, the reason why the object should be ineffable is very much in dispute. On this point the best we can do is to develop a number of categories and evaluate each of them in turn.

Insider Theories

According to one approach, ineffability is not an inherent aspect of the experience or the complex of beliefs leading up to the experience.[9] In this case the problem is basically only that an outsider (the nonmystic) cannot understand what the insider (the mystic) is saying. Those who have not had the experience cannot understand what those who have had it are saying. But once one has experienced the absolute, one knows exactly of what one is speaking, even if others do not comprehend it.

The advantage of the insider theory lies in its coherence with the basic epistemological model of mysticism. If mystical experience is an experience of direct awareness, then someone who has not had that awareness cannot know the content of the experience. A person who has been blind from birth cannot know the color red.

But the insider theory also has a serious disadvantage. It simply does not comport with what many mystics are saying. Their frequent claim is that their experience is inherently incapable of being expressed with words. Many mystics state not just that only the initiated can understand their language but that no language can do justice to their experience. This position makes the problem of ineffability wider than the gap between insider and outsider.

---

[8]J. Kellenberger, "The Ineffabilities of Mysticism," *American Philosophical Quarterly* 16 (1979): 307.

[9]See Daya Krishan, "Mysticism and the Problem of Intelligibility," *Journal of Religion* 34 (1954): 101–5; Hatab, "Mysticism and Language," 51–64.

Limits-of-Language Theory

It is possible to hold that the ineffability in mysticism is only a temporary condition. When mystics wish to tell about their experience, words fail them. They have never had such a thing happen to them before, so they have never been in a position to learn the appropriate language. But that deficiency does not necessitate our saying that no language could ever be used to describe their experience. They and other people could now converse about their experience, perhaps at first in circumlocutions, but later with a newly established vocabulary and grammar. In other words, there really is no ineffability.[10]

This theory is closely related to the insider theory in that it does not posit a fundamental barrier between mysticism and language. But in this case the possibility of communication is not confined to the mystics only, the "insiders." In principle, anyone can learn the language.

There is a clear practical advantage to this theory. After all, it can be demonstrated that something along this line is constantly happening. For example, someone may have had a mystical experience and may try to express what happened in very deficient terms. Someone else who had a similar thing occur may say, "Ah, you had a mystical experience." From this point on, the term "mystical experience" is a meaningful expression referring to this kind of event. Furthermore, a third person who has not had the experience but who has read William James on the matter, can also have a basic understanding of what the expression means. Thus we can see how a deficiency in language can be overcome through the process of building language.

But once again the disadvantages of this explanation seem to outweigh the apparent advantages. The analysis of the

---

[10]Cf. Peter C. Appleby, "Mysticism and Ineffability," *International Journal for Philosophy of Religion* 11 (1980): 143–65. Appleby argues that the so-called problem of ineffability lies in the fact that mysticism yields, not new information, but a new way of seeing things.

problem and the suggested solution are too simple for what most mystics say about ineffability. Certainly the expression "mystical experience" does not capture all that a mystic would like (but is unable) to convey by language. In fact, here is the real nub of the problem. The mystic does not usually deny that one could in a pinch coin enough expressions to circumscribe whatever one needs to express. The real difficulty for the mystic is that such attempts never truly express what he or she would like to say. Once again, the nature of the ineffability is not merely that one is temporarily unable to find the right words, but that it seems ultimately impossible to do so, if the mystic is to be believed.

Lack-of-Concept Theory

The preceding discussion leads us to an apparently inescapable conclusion: It is the concepts underlying language that are deficient. Human concepts simply are inadequate to do justice to the mystical experience. In the area of mysticism, human experience has outdistanced human thought.[11]

Let us be clear on the distinction between this theory and the limits-of-language theory. When the deficiency is only in language, it seems to be redeemable. We can always come up with new words or new ways of using old words. But if the problem is with the concepts underlying language, something cannot be meaningfully asserted because it cannot even be thought in the first place. Thus, as far as language goes, all kinds of things can be said (in the sense of vocalized) about the absolute, but nothing can truly be affirmed. Dionysius the Areopagite stated,

[11]See Gary K. Pletcher, "Mysticism, Contradiction, and Ineffability," *American Philosophical Quarterly* 10 (1973): 201–11; B. Matilal, "Mysticism and Reality: Ineffability," *Journal of Indian Philosophy* 3 (1975): 217–52; Hattiangadi, "Why Is Indian Religion Mystical?" 253–58; Robert Hoffman, "Logic, Meaning, and Mystical Intuition," *Philosophical Studies* 11 (1960): 65–70; Richard H. Jones, "Experience and Conceptualization in Mystical Knowledge," *Zygon* 18 (1983): 139–65.

> We maintain that He is neither soul nor intellect, nor has
> He imagination, opinion, reason, or understanding, nor can
> He be expressed or conceived, since He is neither number,
> nor order, nor greatness, nor smallness, nor equality, nor
> inequality, nor similarity, nor dissimilarity; neither is He
> standing, nor moving, nor at rest; neither has He power, nor
> is power, nor is light; neither does He live, nor is He life;
> neither is He essence, nor eternity, nor time; . . . neither is
> He darkness nor light, nor the false, nor the true; nor can
> any affirmation or negation be applied to Him.[12]

Everything can be said, and nothing can be said. Everything said is true, and yet everything is false because it does not actually apply. We have simply penetrated to a level beyond the concepts of our understanding.

Now this theory has the advantage of actually comporting with what the mystics are saying in all of its radicality. Not all mystics are saying this much, but it is hard to find someone who says anything more extreme. Ineffability is truly absolute because rational concepts have been transcended.

The disadvantage of this view is twofold. First, there is the paradox pointed out by Alston. Mystics who say that the absolute is ineffable are contradicting themselves. They are saying what, as minimal as it may be, cannot be said. By rights, if the lack-of-concept theory is true, mystics ought not to be able to say anything. But they do. Mystics have said much about what cannot be said.

Now many people have not seen Alston's critique as posing a serious drawback. They would concede that mystics appear to violate their own assertions of ineffability—but only if we assume that they are actually affirming anything with their speech. Many would contend, however, that this assumption represents a misunderstanding of the nature of the mystic's language: the best way to understand the language of the mystic is to accept that it is noncognitive.

Noncognitive language is the kind of language that does

---

[12]Dionysius the Areopagite, "The Mystical Theology," in Happold, *Mysticism*, 217.

not purport to represent states of affairs. Examples would be such exclamations as "What a beautiful sunset!" or "Ouch, that hurts!" These kinds of statements are not assertions of anything being true; they are exclamations of personal feelings or impressions. Perhaps they imply cognitive propositions ("There is a sunset"; "There is a cause of pain"), but they themselves are noncognitive. Much philosophy of the first half of this century has been devoted to deciding what kinds of statements are cognitive. The logical positivists led the charge with allowing only statements that resemble scientific ones to count as cognitive. But one does not have to go to such extremes either to recognize the existence of noncognitive statements or to conclude that mystical language could be included in that class.

Calling mystical language noncognitive appears to be helpful. On this account a mystic may say much; but the language surrounding the absolute, that which is supposed to be ineffable, affirms nothing. It expresses feelings, emotions, attitudes, aesthetic judgments, and many other subjective nuances, but it does not convey any factual information.

But here we have the second disadvantage to the lack-of-concepts theory. It would be next to impossible to prove that mystics do not think they are conveying information when they speak of the absolute. Even when they say apparently contradictory things, or when they say that the absolute is ineffable, they still do think that they are imparting information to us. They, at least, seem to believe that their language is cognitive.

This fact is recognized by James when he makes "noetic quality" the second characteristic of mysticism, right after ineffability.[13] It may seem highly paradoxical, but to return to Johnson's figure of speech, Jacob, having seen the unutterable, will insist on making utterances about it. Mystics will think nothing of telling us about that for which they supposedly lack the rational concepts.

---

[13]James, *Varieties*, 300.

Limits-of-Logic Theory

Once again we find ourselves driven from one theory to another. The upshot of the lack-of-concepts theory is a strong suggestion of illogicality. Thus some writers have advocated a theory of ineffability due to illogic.[14]

When we say "illogic," that expression is not strictly fair or accurate. Such writers would claim actually that logic has been transcended; it no longer applies. Even this statement needs further qualification. Let us say that traditional logic does not apply, where by "traditional logic" we mean the system of thought based on the laws of identity $(A = A)$, contradiction (not [A and not-A]) and excluded middle (A or not-A). Whereas in traditional logic a statement and its denial are mutually exclusive, such need not be the case in mysticism, according to this claim.

The limits-of-logic theory comes in two types: the outright denial of logic, and the suggestion of a new and different logic. W. T. Stace represents the first variety. He begins his analysis by establishing a distinct function for logic, namely, the discrimination of one thing from another. But the mystical experience is of the One, a pure undifferentiated unity. Thus logic cannot apply; no discrimination is called for or even possible. The experience itself is not tied to logic, and thus, "the language is only paradoxical because the experience is paradoxical." Consequently, Stace argues that actually the language is literal and the concepts are appropriate. "The language which he finds himself compelled to use is, when at its best, the literal truth about his experience, but it is contradictory."[15] Thus the solution to this whole riddle of ineffability would lie in the lack of logicality within the experience itself.

The problem with this type of the limits-of-logic theory

---

[14]Stace, *Mysticism and Philosophy*, 277–306; John Findlay, "The Logic of Mysticism," *Religious Studies* 2 (1966): 145–62.

[15]Stace, *Mysticism and Philosophy*, 304–5.

has been pointed out by Wainwright.[16] Wainwright has challenged Stace either to make clearer why mystical experience should be exempt from logic or to accept the fact that the mystic's statements are not just peculiar but false. As far as the first half of this disjunction goes, it seems evident that the mystic has not abandoned all distinction in favor of pure undifferentiation. The mystic distinguishes the absolute from the nonabsolute, ultimate experience from normal experience, and so forth. It is impossible to make an absolute case for the inapplicability of logic. But then illogical statements must suffer the same fate in mysticism as illogical statements in other areas of life. When I say that the wheels on my car are both round and square, I am uttering a contradiction. But as every beginning student of logic learns, contradictions are always false. Thus the view of Stace and others would have to lead to interpreting statements made by mystics as not just unusual but false.

Other proponents of the limits-of-logic theory have seen this point and have developed the second type of theory accordingly. Here it is not argued that all logic is transcended by mystical experience, but only so-called common logic. Mysticism has a logic of its own. A statement along that line has the obvious advantage of being both redemptive and conciliatory. It is exactly what the mystic wants and needs to hear. But the scholar is left without help, for the problem persists of what exactly mystical logic is supposed to be.

Consider John Findlay's treatment of this matter. He argues that mysticism has its own logic. It is a logic based on an absolute that is "superlative, self-explanatory and all explanatory, which rounds off all our concepts and valuations and provides the necessary background for all of them." Given this stipulation, within the context of the absolute there can be a genuine consistency, thus a logic. In fact, what would appear as the original weakness of mystical logic, the deprecation of distinctions, becomes its strength, as all distinctions

---

[16]Wainwright, "Stace and Mysticism," 140.

are one in the absolute. But can this mystical logic be understood by the nonmystic? Findlay does not allow that it can, and in the process makes a very telling affirmation: "The theorems of mysticism can only be understood with passion; one must oneself live through, consummate the identity which they postulate."[17]

Thus we are back to the insider theory. The limits-of-logic theory has brought us full circle to our point of origin. Again we need to be mystics before we can know what a mystic is saying. Positing a special logic does not solve the problem of ineffability either.

Evaluation of the Theories

When we indicated above the advantages of all of the theories, this praise was more than mere courtesy or lip service. Each of the theories makes a solid positive contribution to the study of mysticism, even if none of them is completely accurate. Let us review what they say.

The insider theory emphasizes the fact that an outsider can have only a limited understanding of what a mystic is saying. It locates ineffability in the phenomenon that only those who have an inside track can express what otherwise is unintelligible. The limits-of-language theory blames the ineffability on the fact that such an unusual experience has not yet been able to be expressed in words, but it may be later. In opposition, according to the lack-of-concepts theory, language will never catch up because human beings simply do not have the faculties to express their mystical experiences. Finally, the limits-of-logic theory replies that, though we may have the concepts, the ineffability is due to the fact that logic goes awry in mysticism. Thus we have the four results of the four theories:

1. Insiders claim special understanding.
2. Language is inadequate.

---

[17]Findlay, "Logic of Mysticism," 153, 155.

3. Concepts are deficient.
4. Logic is peculiar.

Given those characteristics, Alston seems surely right in speaking of a paradox of ineffability. Any attempt by the mystic to speak at all must be self-defeating. Upon analysis, mysticism and a meaningful use of language seem to be mutually exclusive.

At this point we ought to begin to wonder if maybe the theoretical analysis has not outrun practical realities. After all, it would not be the first time that something like this has happened.

One case in point is the so-called problem of other minds. We experience ourselves as beings with minds and normally also regard other people in the same way. If called on, however, to make a case for other people's having minds like ours instead of just being robots, we may not be able to collect sufficient evidence to mount a convincing argument. Yet very few people would hold the peculiar belief of solipsism—that theirs is the only mind in the world.[18]

More closely related to our present discussion is the study of hermeneutics, the modern science of interpretation. Schleiermacher summed up the dilemma in this area with the following statement: "One must already know a man in order to understand what he says, and yet one first becomes acquainted with him by what he says."[19] The point is this: whenever people say or write anything, they bring to bear all of their background, culture, influences, personality, and so on; and their language is derived from their life world. They will differ significantly from their hearers or readers in these aspects. So how can anyone who d es not derive his or her concepts from the same life world understand what other speakers or writers are saying? Again, if we pursue this line of thought long enough, we may despair of any human being ever

---

[18]See Alvin Plantinga, *God and Other Minds* (Ithaca, N.Y.: Cornell University Press, 1967).
[19]Schleiermacher, *Hermeneutics* 56.

communicating with another one. But we do communicate. In practice we do something that seems to be impossible in theory.

Now it may just be that the language of the mystic constitutes another such bumble-bee issue (named after the insect that is not supposed to be able to fly on technical grounds, but it does anyway). Alston's paradox notwithstanding, mystics do talk, and they do communicate—inside and outside their circles. To do justice to the situation, we need to keep in mind that it is the mystics who have claimed ineffability. But they evidently do not mean (or are mistaken in) the sometimes very extravagant statements they make. Despite all arguments for ineffability, clearly mystical experience is not totally ineffable. Alston would like mystics to qualify their assertions of ineffability in theory. In practice this has been done many times over.

So let us consider this issue in reverse. Rather than starting with the fact of ineffability and then wondering about how it is that mystics still do talk, let us now begin with mystical talk and then see where ineffability fits in.

Mysticism and Other Perceptions

Let us consider the following three statements:

1. The grass is green.
2. God is just and holy.
3. All things are one in the absolute.

Sentence 3 represents a statement typically made by mystics. Number 1 is a statement of empirical perception, and 2 can stand as just one of many things one might say in a religious, but not necessarily mystical, context. Our thesis is that: 3 has significant traits in common with 1 and 2 and is different as a type of language from 1 and 2 in degree only.

Let us begin by examining the first statement. Someone uttering this statement is presumably reporting an observation. It communicates a fact that most people would have little difficulty comprehending. Someone would not understand the statement who was blind, color blind to the extent that color distinctions were meaningless, or not familiar with the language used. Such cases could be considered clearly recognizable exceptions.

The experience of perceiving a certain color is private. Interestingly, there is no way one can really test someone's color perception for what is actually seen. First of all, we cannot look into people's brains to see what they are perceiving. But for practical purposes there are ways of testing some perceptions. In the case of shape perceptions, for example, we can have someone reproduce the shape that he or she has seen in a drawing. For colors, however, all that one can check on is consistency. Let us say that persons A and B both report seeing green. Theoretically it could be the case that, if they saw each other's perceptions, they would call those colors red, that what A calls green, B calls red, and vice versa. But we would never know that this difference in the perception exists, since they both refer to the same object (e.g. grass), as green.[20]

The lesson here is simple, if not inane. No one can test what I actually perceive when I see a color. But it is not necessary for anyone else to have my experience, private though it may be, in order for me to communicate my color perception in language. To demand otherwise would be not so much pedantic as philosophically illiterate.

Now we can make a few comments on sentence 2, a religious assertion. Two properties, justice and holiness, are attributed to God. This kind of proposition has come under considerable philosophical fire over the ages. Much turmoil was created in this century by the logical positivists with their verifiability principle, the statement that a proposition is meaningful only if it is in principle empirically verifiable. Thereby all religious language was consigned to the realm of

---

[20]My thanks to Mark Cosgrove of the Psychology Department of Taylor University for his insights on this point.

meaninglessness or technical nonsense. Logical positivism could not sustain itself for very long, however. First, it became increasingly embarrassing that the verifiability principle itself was not empirically verifiable. Second, positivistic philosophy notwithstanding, people using religious language as part of their life world did not find it to be in the least meaningless.

There has been a much longer tradition of questioning the meaning of religious language from within religious traditions themselves. Some of this internal critique came from mystical elements, but the same concerns were also raised by those whom we would not identify as representatives of mysticism. For example, Thomas Aquinas states that our language about God should properly be considered equivocal, since the words cannot possibly mean the same thing applied to the infinite as to the finite.[21] Thus it would appear that the only appropriate language about God is negative, namely, language that denies limitations of God but does not affirm any positive qualities of him.[22]

Nonetheless, few religious thinkers, including Aquinas, will settle for simply consigning themselves to silence or negative talk. The vast majority of them have explained the meaningfulness of religious language by invoking some sort of set of principles that combines the negative ineffable aspect with positive communicability.

Consider, for example, Aquinas's own solution, in which language about God is considered to be analogical.[23] Analogy always implies a similarity and a difference, and this is also true of language about finite things compared to language about God. On the one hand there is the univocal concept according to which there is some basic similarity; in other words, the love of God and the love of human beings cannot be diametrically opposed to each other in meaning. On the other hand, there is the equivocal predication of the concept. Because God is infinite, anything said of him must differ

---

[21]Thomas Aquinas, *Summa Theologica* 1.4.3, 1.12.7, 1.12.12.
[22]Thomas Aquinas, *Summa contra Gentiles* 1.14.
[23]Thomas Aquinas, *Summa Theologica* 1.13.

qualitatively and quantitatively from the same thing said of creatures.[24] In this aspect analogy retains a certain amount of equivocation. The human meaning can never exhaust the divine meaning.

Now it appears that proposition 3 is not really all that different from 2. Again there is the same kind of interplay between univocity and equivocation. Univocally, we do know a root meaning for the words "things," "one," "absolute," and so forth. Even to the totally uninitiated the words do mean something. Of course the mystic's meaning is different— quantitatively and qualitatively—but not completely different with no common meaning whatsoever.

Thus a plausible conclusion to this matter is that the oddities of mystical language need to be understood by way of analogy, as is the case with other religious language—no more and no less. Alston is surely right with the arguments mentioned at the beginning of this chapter. Utter ineffability is neither demonstrable nor assertable. But claims to ineffability are also exaggerated and overanalyzed. The alternative to ineffability is not exhaustive understanding. It is understanding by way of analogy, where some meaning is conveyed and some further intended meaning may not be conveyed properly. This feature, we must remember, is true of all human communication.

---

[24]See Geisler and Corduan, *Philosophy of Religion*, 252–71; Winfried Corduan, *Handmaid to Theology* (Grand Rapids: Baker, 1981), 95–111.

6

Mysticism in Christendom

IN THIS CHAPTER WE MOVE FORWARD TO CONSIDER the question of compatibility between Christianity and mysticism. We can begin by acknowledging the many and diverse ways in which people have sought to accommodate the two. Since the body of literature is far too large to attempt a comprehensive description of all Christian mysticism, we must be selective in treating various representatives.

Furthermore, the inquiry can make sufficient progress only if our principle of selectivity takes on a negative edge. We shall look at particular traditions specifically with an eye toward some of their theological or philosophical deficiencies. It is to be hoped that in the process we will also be able to glean some of the positive contributions they have made. But a lifetime would not suffice to appropriate all of the good insights that have come from these believers. To be able to come eventually to a conclusion, we have to maintain our critical concerns so that we can move beyond various traditions in order to develop a point of view that is acceptable to our criteria of truth.

In this phase of the inquiry I summarize some of the major Christian mystical traditions. Then we can review what appear to be serious shortcomings in each tradition. In chapter 7, then, I make positive use of our negative conclusions by reconstructing a mystical position on the basis of the New Testament.

Eastern Orthodoxy

A strong mystical tradition within Christendom is found within Eastern Orthodoxy. In fact, if we accept the suggestion made at the outset and define mysticism in terms of its total system rather than on the basis of experience, we could even say that most of Orthodox theology is by nature mystical. At the core of this theology lies the notion of *theosis*—the deification of the human being.

Vladimir Lossky has provided a very helpful summary of Eastern Orthodox theology.[1] Let us follow his insights by inserting them into the four components of our expanded definition of mysticism (see chapter 2).

The Nature of Reality

The distinctiveness of the doctrine of God in Eastern Orthodoxy can be seen most clearly in its approach to the Trinity. In theology proper Lossky argues for the deliberate submission of the intellect to the insoluble paradoxes of theology. Thus he repudiates Western Trinitarian models as rationalistic and relational. One ought never to forget that the three-in-one-ness of God is indeed an incomprehensible mystery and at root incommunicable (44–48).

Thus there can be no question of knowing the essence of God. Nonetheless it is possible to encounter God, but not in his essential nature. God's nature is beyond rationality and even beyond duality. But it is God's energies that interact with the world. According to Lossky, "The distinction is that between the essence of God, or His nature, properly so-called, which is inaccessible, unknowable and incommunicable; and

---

[1]Vladimir Lossky, *The Mystical Theology of the Eastern Church* (Cambridge: Clark, 1944). Hereafter in this section, page citations refer to Lossky's work.

the energies of divine operations, forces proper to and insepa-
rable from God's essence, in which He goes forth from
Himself, manifests, communicates, and gives Himself" (70).
But God is still himself in the energies. Although there is this
distinction between energies and essence, Lossky calls this
distinction "ineffable" (86, 88).

Thus God extends himself to creation through his energies. Lossky cautions against the term "supernatural" in this
connection because he sees a progression in God's relation to
his work (88). There is no pure nature apart from grace (101).

The Self

Just as there is a mystery in the relationship between the
one nature and the three persons in the Trinity, so Lossky sees
a mystery in the one nature and many persons in humanity
(121). The person is not just a small expression of this
overwhelming nature but is free to renounce any nature-
determinism; through an act of renunciation the person can be
freed from the shackles of his or her humanity and thus be
open to the divine energies. As already indicated above, we
cannot really consider a human person in isolation without
immediately taking God's grace into account. Lossky includes
humans in his statement that "created beings have the faculty
of being assimilated to God because such was the very object
of their creation" (101–2).

The Link

Given the Christian context, a link to God is understood
by Lossky in terms of divine grace. The work of grace is the
deification *(theosis)* of the human being, which occurred first
in the Incarnation. Lossky revives the ancient slogan "God
became man in order that man might become god" (134).

To understand this position, we need to pull together
some of the points made above.

The single human nature. In the Incarnation, Christ

deified human nature as he assumed it through the hypostatic union (the union of two natures) in his person.

Our freedom as persons. Since we are not bound to our fallen human nature, we can turn in our persons to God and thereby let human nature as it is found in us be deified as well.

The divine energies. Because God communicates himself through his energies, a human being can thereby actually become deified. We do not become essentially divine, but our nature is assimilated to God by way of the energies. It is in this way that Lossky understands 2 Peter 1:4 to "participate in the divine nature."

Deification is a process, not an instantaneous event. It would probably be fair to Lossky to distinguish the following stages:

1. deification of human nature in the Incarnation;
2. provision of the means of our deification at Pentecost;
3. deification of the person in principle as one becomes a Christian (at baptism);
4. increase in the person's deification over a lifetime;
5. full deification of the person in heaven.

The Experience

Lossky minimizes the typical mystical experience in Eastern Orthodox theology. In fact, he cites with approval St. Symeon the New Theologian, according to whom, "ecstasies and ravishments are appropriate only to beginners and novices—whose nature has not yet gained experience of the uncreated" (209). Thus the mystical experience is not seen as the apex of the Christian life (as it sometimes is in other traditions). It is not denied, but it is evaluated as an immature stage.

At the same time, Eastern Orthodoxy also does not go along with the negative experiences that are an important part of the Latin tradition (see St. John of the Cross and the "dark night of the soul"). Lossky says, "Grace will make itself known as joy, peace, inner warmth and light. . . . Dryness is a state of illness which must not last, it is never thought of by the mystical writers of the Eastern tradition as a necessary and normal stage in the way of union" (225). Thus the person truly on the way toward God's full work in him or her will live neither in ecstasy nor despair but in a state of rest and equilibrium.

Response to Eastern Orthodox Mysticism

By way of response, we can make the following critical observations. The first four points are positive, the last one is negative.

Eastern Orthodoxy is concerned with realities, not experiences. Experiences are not entirely ruled out, but they are at best given inferior status to the basic reality of *theosis*.

Eastern Orthodoxy has maintained a theistic view of God. Despite the tendency of many mystics to get lost in pantheism, this is not the case for Eastern Orthodoxy. The Trinitarian personal God, who is both transcendent and immanent, is in evidence here.

Eastern Orthodoxy emphasizes God's direct action. Even though Lossky wants to avoid the term "supernatural," still in contrast to a naturalistic worldview, that is what this theology is—and proudly so. Western liberal theologies have tried to eliminate the supernatural from Christianity. Even more conservative writers seem to concentrate their studies of the Christian life on motivation, effort, and technique. But Eastern Orthodoxy rightly begins with God's unmediated work, which comes through his own energies.

Eastern Orthodoxy emphasizes God's grace. We are going to see how other Christian mystics understand the Christian life as an unceasing struggle. In such a setting "grace" would mean no more than "reward." But Eastern Orthodoxy makes a strong case for the gratuitousness of God's work.

But Eastern Orthodoxy seems to minimize sin and reconciliation. Perhaps as a Westerner, I cannot see all of the ramifications of *theosis*. Certainly scriptural statements, such as 2 Peter 1:4, deserve the same consideration as other passages. But it is very hard to turn this verse into the fundamental principle of the Gospel. To what extent there is such a thing as *theosis* need not be decided here (see the discussion on the indwelling of the Holy Spirit in the next chapter). It suffices at this point to indicate the absence of New Testament salvation theology in Lossky. We need to affirm that at the core of the New Testament message is the belief that each human being is a fallen sinner who needs to come to personal faith in Jesus Christ so as to be reconciled to God. In contrast, Eastern Orthodox theology seems to treat sin only as a deficiency that is then overcome in the process of becoming like God. Lossky goes so far as to state, "One can say that in a certain sense the work of Christ was a preparation for that of the Holy Spirit. . . . Pentecost is thus the object, the final goal, of the divine economy upon earth" (159). It looks as though Lossky may be guilty of minimizing the importance of Christ's atonement in its own right and of reversing Christ's statement that the work of the Holy Spirit is to glorify him (John 16:12–16).

Early Western Mysticism

Dom Cuthbert Butler calls early medieval mysticism "Western" mysticism, in distinction to later "Latin" mysticism. His study of this particular phenomenon includes Augustine, Gregory, and Bernard and thereby excludes such medieval mystics as Meister Eckhart and Teresa of Ávila as belonging to a later, distinct movement. He lists the following points as distinctive for the mysticism in this classification: [2]

1. It occurred prior to the scholastic period.
2. It is not characterized by negation or obscurity but is a positive experience of God.

---

[2]Butler, *Western Mysticism*, 179–86.

3. It is not accompanied by separate visions and revelations.
4. It never includes acts of bodily violence.
5. It is free of other psychophysiological accompaniments.
6. The mystics in this category were not afraid of diabolical intrusions or satanic counterfeits.

As one representative of this group, let us take a look at Augustine and the two experiences he relates in his *Confessions*. He places the first of these two experiences at the time period before he had his complete conversion in the garden.[3] At this time Augustine was essentially convinced of the truth of Christianity but was unable to bring himself to a positive decision to follow Christ. As is evident from the description, however, he definitely had already made a conversion to Neoplatonism.

This first vision is something of an intellectual experience in the sense that it describes an inner journey taken by Augustine. Beginning with the observation of the physical universe, he finds that he passes intellectual judgment on various states of affairs. But he would not be able to do so if there were no immutable and eternal truth beyond all changeable things and minds. Thus Augustine sets out on a spiritual progression that takes him from the senses to the constancy of truth. Finally he recognizes the total preferability of the immutable, which lies beyond all of those categories. And thus, for one brief moment, he had a quick glimpse of "that which is," namely, pure unchanging being—God.

A similar pattern underlies the vision that Augustine and his mother, Monica, experienced at Ostia shortly before her death.[4] Again there is an inner journey beginning with the impermanent physical world. Propelled by love, they move up to heaven and inwardly through the mind to the eternal and

---

[3]Augustine, *The Confessions of St. Augustine*, trans. John K. Ryan (Garden City, N.Y.: Doubleday Anchor, 1960), 175, 195–96 (7.23, 8.19–20).
[4]Ibid., 223–24 (9.27–28).

undying being of God. After a time they return once again to the changeable world, but with a new appreciation of its inferiority to the eternal nature of God.

Several points stand out in these descriptions. First, both of Augustine's experiences are heavily determined by his philosophical Neoplatonism. As we ascertained earlier in this study, there is no such thing as a pure experience, so that we can say that Augustine had a specifically Neoplatonic mystical experience.

Second, the target of Augustine's mystical experience is God in one of his essential attributes: immutability. Augustine progresses toward this realization, beginning with God as a reference point for all change in the world. That emphasis does not denigrate other of God's attributes or their importance (e.g. his love or grace), but it does give the description a unique flavor.

Third, the experience is presented as the epitome of Christian experience—even as the epitome of Christianity. There seems to be nothing higher in Augustine's conception than his vision at Ostia. All of the Christian life is focused on this experience, and having reached it, all that is left is its interpretation and influence on the rest of his life. But it is never surpassed.

Fourth, the experience results in a view of the created world as decidedly inferior. Augustine mentions with approval how after the experience Monica "talked . . . about contempt of this life and the advantages of death." And again after her death, Augustine is very critical of his grief. He confesses that "it distressed me greatly that these human feelings had a sway over me."[5] In short, the Augustinian mystical experience turns out to be strongly world-denying at the same time as it is God-affirming.

Let us, then, take Augustine as typical of this brand of "Western" Christian mysticism and make the following assessment. This mysticism intends to be doctrinally ortho-

---

[5]Ibid., 224–25 (9.28).

dox. We do not observe here the questionable beliefs of later traditions, which at least flirt with unorthodox formulations, if not heretical conceptions. The mystical experience is built into theological systems that not only pass the standards of orthodoxy; they *became* the standards of orthodoxy for Western Christianity.

Also, in this form of mysticism, the experience is presented as the epitome of God's work in the life of the believer. Butler states that to question the truth of this form of mysticism would leave the evidently undesirable result that "mysticism would not be the culminating point of religious experience, the last word in the philosophy of religion."[6] But such a statement is theologically problematic. The Bible does not present the mystical experience as the culmination of Christian life or doctrine. Even if for the moment we want to stipulate that Scripture may leave it open as a possibility for the believer, it is certainly not advocated as the highest goal in one's life. Nor are Christians exhorted in the Bible to seek a mystical experience.

Finally, the world-denying quality of Western mysticism, as represented by Augustine, causes difficulty. The New Testament does teach us to retain earthly things in their proper perspective as subordinate to God (Matt. 6:19–21). But the New Testament also states that "everything God created is good" (1 Tim. 4:4) and denounces asceticism (Col. 2:16–23). Nowhere is the injunction not to be conformed to the world interpreted as escape from routine daily living (see 2 Thess. 3:6–13). Thus the tendency to use the mystical experience to promote otherworldliness needs to be resisted theologically.

Meister Eckhart and Later German Mysticism

No discussion on Christian mysticism is complete without reference to Meister Eckhart. And yet it is extremely

---

[6]Butler, *Western Mysticism*, 18.

difficult to pin down exactly what Eckhart meant to say. As Etienne Gilson put it, "The difficulty is not to find a good interpretation of Master Eckhart, but rather to choose between so many consistent interpretations based upon unimpeachable texts, and yet differing among themselves to the point of being contradictory."[7] Could it be that this characteristic of Eckhart interpretations is reflective of Eckhart's writings? While not pretending here to give a definitive statement on Eckhart, we can review some main points and interpretations.

Eckhart's thought is rooted in a Thomistic background, but he makes some unique contributions within it. One is his distinction between God and the Godhead. The Godhead is the very essence of God, beyond all categories and characterizations. He says, "God in the Godhead is spiritual substance, so elemental that we can say nothing about it excepting that it is naught. To say it is aught were more lying than true."[8]

Eckhart also, with many different expressions, teaches about the union of the soul with God. It is these passages that have caused much controversy on his thought. He speaks of the birth of God in the soul.[9] He states that "at the touch of God [the soul] is made uncreaturely."[10] He even asserts, "Henceforth I shall not speak about the soul, for she has lost her name yonder in the oneness of divine essence. There she is no more called soul: she is called infinite being." And again, "She plunges into the bottomless well of the divine nature and becomes one with God that she herself would say that she is God."[11] How should we interpret such statements?

One approach to Eckhart is that taken by Rudolf Otto.[12] Otto sets up a very careful comparison between Eckhart and the Hindu mystic Shankara and finds agreement on all major metaphysical points (e.g. the conceptions of God, the soul,

---

[7]Cited in Master Eckhart, *Parisian Questions and Prologues,* trans. Armand A. Maurer (Toronto: Pontifical Institute of Medieval Studies, 1974), 8.

[8]Meister Eckhart, "Tractate 11," cited in Happold, *Mysticism,* 271.

[9]Meister Eckhart, "Sermon 1," in Happold, *Mysticism,* 276–78.

[10]Meister Eckhart, "Sermon 83," in Happold, *Mysticism,* 276.

[11]Meister Eckhart, "Tractate 2," in Happold, *Mysticism,* 275.

[12]Otto, *Mysticism East and West.*

salvation). The only major difference Otto sees is in the fact that Eckhart's thought issues in an active morality, whereas Shankara leads to quietism. But on this interpretation there is no real difference between Vedantic God-human identity and the teachings of Eckhart. Quotations such as the above on the soul seem to support such a view.

However, the majority of current interpreters favor a different view. For example, Richard Kiekhefer tries to deny anything theologically unusual in Eckhart, except maybe his hyperbolic rhetoric.[13] Kiekhefer's claim is based on a methodology that first of all emphasizes allowing the context of any quotation to determine as conservative an interpretation as possible and using Eckhart's deliberately paradoxical statements as a clue that they are intended as exaggeration, not as ordinary, factual statements.

Kiekhefer makes some important distinctions. First he differentiates between three types of union between God and the soul in the wider world of Christian mysticism: (1) habitual—the indwelling of God by grace in the believer, a given reality; (2) ecstatic—a special experience, as exemplified by Paul in 2 Corinthians 12:1–6; and (3) unitive life— a prolonged state of ecstatic union. A second distinction is between abstractive and nonabstractive union. Abstractive union turns away from the reality and consciousness of everyday life, whereas nonabstractive union does not.[14]

In Otto's assessment, Eckhart advocates ecstatic and abstractive union, which leads to a unitive, nonabstractive life. But Kiekhefer gives his "inescapable conclusion" that "Eckhart did not view ecstatic or abstractive union with God as integral to the life of the soul, or even a goal to be sought or particularly treasured. The state to which he invites his reader is that of habitual and nonabstractive union; he nowhere says that other forms are necessary or even helpful in the attainment of that goal." Kiekhefer's point is that Eckhart used

---

[13]Kiekhefer, "Meister Eckhart's Conception," 203–25.
[14]Ibid., 204.

excessive language in order to sell, not a new and different experience, but the validity of the kind of experience accessible even to the humblest Christian.[15]

One wonders if the correct interpretation of Eckhart may not lie somewhere between Otto and Kiekhefer. Kiekhefer's study is based on a solid foundation of textual research. The trouble with Kiekhefer's position, however, is that many of Eckhart's contemporaries, both friends and foes, understood Eckhart more in line with Otto's assessment, leading eventually to certain official condemnations. It remains the case that, if Eckhart had said only ordinary things, he might not even be studied today, and if he meant to say only ordinary things, he certainly did not help his cause.

In any event, if an interpretation like Otto's is right, we do not have to look far to find fault with Eckhart's thought. Orthodox Christian theology has no room for either pantheism or a doctrine of the uncreated divine nature of the soul.

On the other hand, if Kiekhefer is correct in his interpretation of Eckhart, then there appears to be little to quarrel with. A habitual nonabstractive union with God ought to occupy an important place in Christian theology, a point to which we must return in the next chapter. If this is what Eckhart intended to teach, we can learn some important lessons from him when we draw our own conclusions.

It remains to point out one significant question about Eckhart from the vantage point of a modern evangelical Christian. Armand A. Maurer finds it necessary to defend Eckhart against incipient Protestantism.[16] This reaction may have been brought about by Otto, who saw some similarities between Eckhart and Martin Luther. Otto states, "The relationship between the mystical thought of Eckhart and the doctrines of Justification and Grace can be summed up as follows: They run parallel and correspond almost point for

---

[15]Ibid., 224–25.

[16]Armand A. Maurer, *Medieval Philosophy* (New York: Random House, 1962), 303.

point. Further: their terminology is interchangeable."[17] But Maurer protests that Eckhart does not intend to denigrate the role of human works as an aid to salvation, but merely to stress God's grace in making human works acceptable.

On this point Kiekhefer's interpretation supports Maurer's.[18] The experience of union with God is premised on the proper preparation by meeting God's moral prerequisites for us. Only then can we receive that gracious experience of God's birth in our souls. But from the evangelical standpoint, if Maurer is right, then Eckhart is wrong. For then, as a good medieval Christian, he falls short of our understanding of God's free grace and our justification as a declaration by God based on Christ's righteousness alone, not ours. Thus we see Eckhart, at least on conservative interpretations, as teaching a very modest form of mysticism, but within a truncated view of grace. On the more radical interpretation, his understanding of grace may become more congenial, but the mystical system as a whole then becomes unpalatable.

St. Teresa and St. John of the Cross

Let us examine St. Teresa of Ávila and St. John of the Cross as representatives of later Latin mysticism. The writings of these two monastic reformers are known for their colorful descriptions of the union of the soul with Jesus. They have influenced Christian mysticism to such an extent that their expositions have bordered on becoming standard for Christendom.[19]

Consider, for example, Teresa's four degrees of prayer, which she likens to various ways in which a garden may be watered. These are, first, *drawing water out of a well*. The person praying relies on his or her understanding. There is much effort and little reward. Second is *using a windlass to draw the water*. This image stands for the prayer of quiet. The

[17]Otto, *Mysticism East and West*, 211–23, quotation on p. 221.
[18]Kiekhefer, "Meister Eckhart's Conception," 213.
[19]Happold, *Mysticism*, 356.

person enjoys some rest. There is also some reward in terms of peace and satisfaction. Next is *flowing water from a stream or spring*. Now God takes over and provides his bliss directly. The only thing required of the person is to direct the flow. Teresa says, "This state of prayer seems to me a most definite union of the whole soul with God."[20] Yet in contrast to the complete quietism of the second degree, in this stage the soul may also carry out good works. The last way is *rain*: God simply lets his bliss come down on the person directly in a totally overwhelming experience. Teresa claims that in this state "the soul feels that it is not altogether dead, . . .though it is entirely dead to the world." There is great joy. It is so great that "there is no power left in the body—and the soul possesses none—by which this joy can be communicated." This experience may occur after a long period of prayer. Then "the soul is conscious that it is fainting almost completely away in a kind of swoon, with a very great calm and joy." Teresa concludes this description with the double attestation that there is no room for any doubt in this experience, but admits, "Nor can I myself understand this."[21]

John of the Cross is well known for his tripartite division of the mystic way: the ways of purgation, illumination, and union.[22] Another important element of his description of the mystic way is the "dark night of the soul," a time of purification in preparation for the final union.[23] First, there is the dark night of the senses in which the soul simply learns to contemplate. Second, there is the spiritual purgation necessary for the climax of the mystical experience. John provides three reasons for a concept of this dark night.

1. Renunciation and deprivation. The soul must be freed from all worldly attachments.
2. Faith. The soul cannot rely on its reason, but must

---

[20]St. Teresa, *Life*, in Happold, *Mysticism*, 350.
[21]Ibid., 351–54.
[22]See the brief description in chapter 2 above.
[23]St. John of the Cross, "Ascent of Mount Carmel," in Happold, *Mysticism*, 358.

travel by way of faith, which he describes as "as dark as night to the understanding."[24]

3. God. For God also is unknowable to finite humans. Only when the soul has been purged through this negative experience is it capable of the ultimate rapture of union with Christ.

As typical representatives of later Latin mysticism, Teresa and John correctly emphasize a supernatural experience with God. As in their day they sought to provide an alternative to a dry and worldly monasticism, their exuberance is also needed at many other times and places—whenever the church has fallen into formalism and superficiality. But in many other ways their descriptions are open to serious questioning. Specifically, there are problems with authority and grace.

John and Teresa refer freely to Bible passages but still make their own experiences normative whenever they find it convenient to do so. This is not to say that all of their ideas are contrary to Scripture, but that they do not seem to submit their experiences to scriptural judgment. This deficiency could be one of the causes of their troubles with the Inquisition. Along this line, the Christian wishing to learn from them cannot get around the question of why, if this experience is the culmination of the Christian life, the union and the way to achieve it are not taught more clearly in the Bible.

Teresa and John do not equate the experience of union with salvation, though it is not easy to see where it is intended to fit in a traditional theological scheme. The fault here may lie largely with such schemata. Nonetheless, a Protestant will once again insist that the role of grace in God's ways with humanity has been usurped here by a notion of reward. Though both writers insist on God's love and grace as the reason for the bliss bestowed on us, it is really not grace in the strict sense. For only the soul that has passed through the

---

[24]Ibid., 359.

preparatory stages, only the soul that has truly been purged sufficiently of all attachment to the world, receives this boon from God. Thus, whatever the nature of the divine bestowal, it is not God's free gift but at best an exceedingly kind reward.

Recent Writers

There has been a persistent, though minor, strain of mysticism in twentieth-century English language writings on Christian spirituality.[25] They tend to reference each other as authoritative, and they see themselves as standing in the same ancient tradition of mysticism (which is not to say that they actually do say the same things). Here a few generalizations must suffice, using a few comments from Evelyn Underhill and others as examples.

These writers tend to subscribe to some form of the unanimity argument; that is, they accept the notion of mysticism as a perennial philosophy, though they differentiate between purer and not-so-pure forms. The highest form of mysticism is located within Christianity. Nevertheless, Underhill defines mysticism as the apprehension of "Reality," of which Christian reality is a particular case.[26]

They are divided on the question of whether Jesus was a mystic or not. Underhill thinks he was and that he manifested all of the standard phases of the life of the mystic.[27] His highest mystical experiences occurred at his baptism, transfiguration, and resurrection. But Harkness disagrees; she does not "think that we can say that Jesus was a mystic."[28]

They agree that John and Paul were mystics. Underhill summarizes John's description of the life of Jesus: "He saw in that career the clear emergence in the Here-and-Now of the

---

[25]E.g. Butler, *Western Mysticism;* Georgia Harkness, *Mysticism: Its Meaning and Message* (Nashville: Abingdon, 1973); Inge, *Christian Mysticism;* Rufus M. Jones, *Some Exponents of Mystical Religion* (Nashville: Abingdon, 1930); Underhill, *Mysticism;* Underhill, *Mystic Way.*
[26]Underhill, *Mystic Way.*
[27]Ibid., 73–82.
[28]Harkness, *Mysticism,* 42.

Divine Nature; the sudden and perfect self-expression of the creative Spirit of God, in and through humanity; the path of intensest life mapped out for the race."[29] Similarly Harkness finds the fourth gospel to be thoroughly mystical.[30] W. R. Inge calls it the "Charter of Christian Mysticism."[31]

These recent Christian mystics also find Paul's writings to be full of mysticism. Harkness refers to him as the "first great Christian mystic." She identifies Paul's conversion experience on the Damascus road with his vision of third heaven as reported in 2 Corinthians 12 and treats it as the epitome of mystical experience.[32] Underhill, who considers Jesus to have been a textbook mystic, expounds the life of Paul as following the pattern of Jesus.[33] Adolf Deissmann's conclusion that Paul's phrase "in Christ" is essentially mystical is cited frequently by these writers.[34]

The Bible is not the final authority for these writers. According to Georgia Harkness, "The mystics and devotional writers of the past seldom made a fetish of the Bible, but directly or indirectly were nourished by it."[35] This observation is something of a left-handed compliment. Harkness means to indicate that the Bible has been important for these mystics, but at the same time she states correctly that the Bible is less than supreme divine revelation for them. The position of final authority has been given to mystical experience or mystical tradition.

As a consequence of the last point, one also finds traditional Christian doctrine either missing or reinterpreted in the light of mystical experience in many of these writers.

In sum, there are a number of late-nineteenth and twentieth-century Christian writers who see themselves as

---

[29]Underhill, *Mystic Way*, 221.
[30]Harkness, *Mysticism*, 44–54.
[31]Inge, *Christian Mysticism*, 44; cf. Harkness, *Mysticism*, 49.
[32]Harkness, *Mysticism*, 43.
[33]Underhill, *Mystic Way*, 157–209.
[34]Adolf Deissmann, *Paul: A Study in Social and Religious History* (New York: Harper and Row, 1957).
[35]Harkness, *Mysticism*, 35.

standing in the line of universal mystical tradition, which they see as validly expressed in Christianity. The major flaws in this movement have already been mentioned in connection with other Christian traditions, particularly the shift in authority from the Bible to experience, making experience the epitome of Christian existence and, consequently, minimizing of the gospel of redemption.

Summary

I have given this brief survey of mysticism in Christendom a deliberately negative slant. While such a treatment is not unfair, it is not entirely representative. Some instances of Christian mysticism avoid many of the shortcomings pointed out above. But I am reserving the positive treatment for the next chapter. Here we have surveyed the diversity of Christian mystical expressions and the problems that they engender. Let us bring this chapter to a conclusion by drawing up a catalog of errors to be avoided. The following ideas from mysticism are incompatible with biblical Christianity:

1. Pantheism.
2. Dualism. Any thought form that would deny the reality or significance of the created material world goes counter to Scripture (1 Tim. 4:4).
3. Experience as revelation. A mystical experience may not displace the priority of biblical revelation.
4. Minimizing sin. Many mystical systems, including some Christian ones, begin with the premise that the human person stands already in a relationship to God that only needs to be realized. But biblical Christianity recognizes human fallenness and the need for reconciliation on the basis of the work of Christ.
5. Minimizing grace. Conversely, some Christian forms of mysticism recognize the problem of sin and then lay down rules for personal self-purgation. This approach

is also unbiblical. According to the New Testament, salvation is the free gift of God, received by faith alone.

6. Making a mystical experience central. If the New Testament allows for mystical experience at all, then it can only be at the fringe of Christian experience. We are nowhere taught to seek such an experience, let alone a method to go about procuring one.

With these caveats in mind, we can proceed to the crucial question: Is there a mysticism allowable in the New Testament?

New Testament–Based Mysticism

IN THIS CHAPTER WE SHALL GO BACK TO THE SOURCE to answer the question of whether there is room for mysticism in Christianity. Since the context for this study is evangelical Christianity, the source is the Bible—in particular, the New Testament. And whatever the New Testament teaches on the subject must be considered binding. In a different context, such as one inspired by a demythologization hermeneutic, assertions in the New Testament could possibly be nothing more than expressions of an antiquated Middle Eastern spirituality. But for the evangelical, who considers the Bible to be the authoritative and truthful Word of God, unequivocal statements in the New Testament must speak decisively on the issue. Under this presupposition, then, it would make no sense to distinguish between New Testament mysticism and an acceptable evangelical mysticism.

Some Cautions

Although we considered a number of caveats in the last chapter, we do well to review here a few more.

Normativeness

We need to be clear on what it means to consult the New Testament for standards. There are three traditional categories for such evaluation: (1) things specifically enjoined in Scripture; (2) things specifically forbidden in Scripture; and (3) things neither specifically enjoined nor specifically forbidden in Scripture.

The last category needs some comment. It is not the case that from the New Testament's perspective all beliefs and actions not specifically treated by name are optional for individuals to decide as they see fit. For there are general guidelines to help us adjudicate situations that are not clear one way or the other. For example, the apostle Paul told the Roman Christians that, even though there is nothing intrinsically wrong with eating meat, they should refrain from doing so if it harms another believer spiritually (Rom. 14). In short, some items fitting under this category might yet be considered wrong, whereas others could definitely be permitted.

But it is also easy to slide from something being permitted into making it a standard or ideal for all Christians. Consider the following remarks by George A. Barrois. First he states clearly, "Our faith, and the life which originates in the faith, must measure up to revealed standards. These are found in Scripture, which provides an effective control of mysticism. Any experience, however moving, any conviction, however plausible, becomes suspicious as soon as it cannot possibly be reconciled with the truths or rules found in the Bible."

We can only applaud such a solid statement of biblical authority. However, one page later Barrois affirms,

> The development of mystical experience cannot be disjoined from the progress of faith. It admits of a variety of degrees, from the first moment in which man accepts to be led by the Spirit, to the time of fullness, when the mind comes into the radiance of pure light, when the will is afire

with love, and when the mortal flesh exultantly acknowledges the presence of its Creator and Sustainer.[1]

But where is this experience taught in the New Testament? It is certainly nowhere in the words used by Barrois. Of course it would be theologically naïve as well as contrary to what was said above to think that any experience that is not explicitly prohibited in some verse is incompatible with the Bible. Barrois could reply by saying that this is exactly the kind of experience alluded to by Paul in his prayer of Ephesians 3:14–19 or his vision of 2 Corinthians 12:2–4. Thus Barrois's description would apparently be compatible with the New Testament.

Nevertheless, Barrois's description is not compatible for the following reason: It cannot be ruled out that the experience he describes is permitted by the New Testament. But is it encouraged? The answer is questionable. Is it established as the highest form of Christian experience? Now the answer is definitely negative. Though such an ecstatic experience may be mentioned in the New Testament, it is never set up as a goal for all believers. And yet when Barrois mentions this experience, he calls it the "time of fullness," thereby making it an ideal for all Christians to strive for. And if it is such a universal ideal, then all Christians are actually obligated to pursue it. James 4:17 says that it is a sin for a believer not to do a good thing. Thus if this experience were right for all believers, it would be sinful not to seek the experience. But such a conclusion surely exceeds the New Testament's teaching.

We see here how even in a very carefully argued article, which is very conscious of scriptural authority, it is possible to go beyond the Bible and make an experience normative. No one type of experience is taught in the New Testament as normative. Instead the New Testament's ideal for a Christian life is a state of being in which the will is in complete

---

[1]George A. Barrois, "Mysticism—What Is It?" *Theology Today* 4 (1947): 197–99.

harmony with God's will as the person's status as new creature in Christ is fully realized. Certain subjective states such as joy and peace (and the rest of the fruit of the Holy Spirit) are sent from God, but so may be hardship and suffering (see the experiences of Ezekiel and Jeremiah). How this dynamic works out in the experience of individuals will vary with their personality and specific calling.

Experience and Revelation

William James made the noetic dimension one of the four typical aspects of mystical experience.[2] The significance of this inclusion lies with the idea that mystics believe they have learned something in their experience. They do not think they merely have a feeling, but somehow they come away with some new insight into themselves and the universe (e.g. they suddenly might be convinced that at bottom all things are one). The fact that they may not be able to articulate their insight does not distract from this noetic quality.

Set into the context of the New Testament, this aspect of the mystical experience becomes problematic. For it would entail that mystical experience becomes a source of revelation, a private avenue of insight into God and his workings. If so, as Arthur L. Johnson points out, the evangelical commitment to Scripture as the sole source of revelation becomes undermined. "The Scriptures nowhere teach that God gives us any knowledge through 'spiritual experience.' Knowledge of spiritual matters is always linked to God's propositional revelation, the written Word."[3]

He takes to task Watchman Nee's notion of a spiritual intuition superior to the Bible[4] and A. W. Tozer's "knowledge

---

[2]James, *Varieties*, 300.

[3]Arthur L. Johnson, "Mysticism and Evangelical Thought," *Bulletin of the Evangelical Philosophical Society* 8 (1985): 25. (This article is incorrectly listed under the name of James D. Spiceland.) Cf. Johnson's similar observations in *Faith Misguided*, 30.

[4]Watchman Nee, *The Spiritual Man*, 3 vols. (New York: Christian Fellowship, 1968).

by direct spiritual experience."[5] Johnson argues that any such concept "is effectively to replace the written Word with that mystical experience."[6]

There is much to commend in Johnson's argumentation. He makes the point that a truth supposedly revealed in subjective experience need not necessarily be in conflict with Scripture; it ought also not go beyond Scripture to transcend the evangelical understanding of revelation.[7] He is correct in taking a strong line on this issue, for the very foundation of evangelical doctrine is at stake.

Nonetheless, what he is saying still seems overstated. It seems that Johnson ignores the possibility of a mystical experience that gives a person subjective confirmation of biblical truth. This is undoubtedly what Tozer had in mind. Ideally, a simple biblical statement ought to be sufficient for the believer. Yet at times we have emotional difficulty accepting what the Bible teaches. There is nothing invidious about the idea that at this point God can send us an experience in which he inscribes these written truths on our hearts. No new knowledge is revealed, but a new feeling of certitude about the already-revealed knowledge results.

The danger of mysticism as a source of knowledge is not located where Johnson places it. The problem is not whether we come to know truth through experience but whether the experience and the truth that it points to are wholly subordinate to the Bible. The experience may not reveal different truths from the Bible in the sense of being either in opposition to scriptural teaching or even in addition to the Bible. But it is hard to see how a biblically compatible experience yielding certainty of a biblically revealed truth can be construed as contrary to *sola Scriptura*.

Nonetheless, such an epistemic mysticism is definitely not taught as normative in Scripture. If we intend to find

---

[5]A. W. Tozer, *Man: The Dwelling Place of God* (Harrisburg, Pa.: Christian Publications, 1966), 52.

[6]Johnson, "Mysticism and Evangelical Thought," 19.

[7]Johnson, *Faith Misguided*, 30.

mysticism in the New Testament, we had better look for something less tenuous. In any case, it is probably a mistake to make too much of the noetic dimension of mysticism. Mystical experience as a source of knowledge is important historically but perhaps (pace William James) not a defining characteristic of mysticism. Let us return to our original working definition of mysticism: an unmediated link to an absolute. This definition leaves the epistemic question an open one. In the New Testament we find a state of being, not a way of knowing.

Experience and Theism

Some mystical experiences are monistic; many are not. As we saw earlier, the attempt by Stace and others to find a fundamental monism behind all true mystical experience is to commit a fundamental philosophical error. Many varieties of mysticism (e.g. Sufism or Yoga) are not monistic.

Thus a search for mysticism in a New Testament context need not be a step toward monism. Indeed, how could it be? The New Testament is set into the worldview of theism, which maintains a strict distinction between God and creation, between God and the human being, and between various created entities. All of these named categories are real. Thus the New Testament worldview is pluralistic. If there is mysticism in the New Testament, it cannot be monistic.

This point may seem too obvious to be worth making. But there are two reasons why the above caveat needs to be repeated. First, there is a "slippery-slope" fear today that mysticism leads to pantheism. Arthur L. Johnson speaks disparagingly of mysticism partly because it "is a major force today in the move toward a pantheistic view of God."[8] Needless to say, the approach to mysticism as a perennial philosophy, which sees every mysticism as a monism at heart, is partially to blame for this fear. However, there is no need to

---

[8]Johnson, "Mysticism and Evangelical Thought," 19.

view mysticism in this way. Second, modern pantheistic movements such as New Age have misused Scripture to their own ends. But the problem here is with the perversion of Scripture by imposing a pagan worldview on it. Our analysis has nothing to do with New Age eisegesis. But just as a cultic distortion of the deity of Christ ought not to keep us from investigating that topic, so New Age aberrations ought not to close the door on our appraisal of possibly mystical spirituality in the New Testament. But, does the New Testament teach an unmediated link to God?

Christ the Mediator

At this point a serious potential misunderstanding needs to be cleared up. It is obvious that mediation plays a crucial role in the Bible. Paul states that the Old Testament law was mediated (Gal. 3:19–20). But most important, Jesus Christ is our mediator to God (1 Tim. 2:5). There is no access to God, except through him. Therefore it would appear that no unmediated link to God is possible for us.

This objection rests on a confusion concerning the role of mediation in Christian theology. Jesus Christ is indeed our mediator to God. This ministry of his is the key to our salvation. He brings us into a new position with God, from alienation and condemnation to reconciliation and justification. Whereas before we were strangers, through Christ's mediatorial work we can now be God's children. There is no relationship with God apart from Jesus Christ. I made this point in chapter 6 as a corrective to mistaken notions of Christian mysticism. An experience of God has to be premised on salvation through Jesus Christ, not just on our spiritual capacity.

But to say that this truth closes the door on mystical reality is to miss two important points. First, Jesus Christ himself is God. Christian theology (at least in its orthodox phases) asserts unequivocally the full humanity and full deity of Jesus Christ. Hence the man Jesus, who is our mediator with God, is also God, and a relationship with him must also be a relationship with God. As a matter of fact, much of Christian mysticism has been intentionally Christ-directed. Second, the Christian life does not end at the point of having been reconciled to God; it only begins there. And although the ongoing relationship to God is possible only through the high priesthood of Christ, it has many further dimensions indicated by the New Testament. The believer enjoys a direct relationship with God. Various aspects of this relationship constitute the possible mystical reality for the believer. Let us delineate them further.

The Indwelling of the Holy Spirit

One of the central truths of the New Testament is that believers in Jesus Christ enjoy the very presence of God within them through his Holy Spirit. In John 14:17 Jesus promises the abiding presence of the Spirit. In Romans 8:9 Paul states that to have the Spirit is a mark of belonging to Christ. He refers to the believer's body as the temple of the Holy Spirit (1 Cor. 6:19). These and other similar verses teach this important doctrine.[9] We may make several observations concerning the Spirit's indwelling.

The New Testament understanding of the indwelling of the Holy Spirit is as a reality, not just as metaphor. Kendell H. Easley concludes a study of this subject with the observation, "According to Paul, the Holy Spirit as an entity really lives inside the one who believes in Christ."[10] He contrasts this understanding with a figurative view in which this doctrine is understood as merely expressing a new relationship with God. But through his exegetical efforts he shows that such a view cannot be the case, and he quotes with approval Michael

---

[9]See also Rom. 8:11; 1 Cor. 3:16; 2 Cor. 6:16; 2 Tim. 1:14.

[10]Kendell H. Easley, "To Pneuma tou Theou Oikei en Humin: A Literal Indwelling by the Spirit-as-Substance or a Figurative Reference to a Personal Relationship?" (Paper presented to the Evangelical Theological Society, November 1987), 22.

Green, who writes that Scripture "reveals the deity actually resident within believers, and it is through the Spirit that this takes place. . . . The Spirit comes and takes up residence in a man once he is invited in."[11]

The Holy Spirit indwells all believers. The New Testament sets only one condition for the indwelling of the Spirit, namely, to be a Christian. Romans 8:9 states clearly that if anyone does not have the Spirit of Christ (used synonymously with "the Spirit of God"), that person does not belong to Christ. And of course one comes to belong to Christ through faith in him (Gal. 2:16; Eph. 2:8–9). This fact rules out the idea that someone must have had a particular experience or have achieved a certain level of spirituality prior to enjoying this indwelling. Though the beginning of the indwelling may sometimes be accompanied by an unusual experience (see Acts 19:1–6), none is ever stipulated as a necessary precondition.

One of the purposes of the indwelling of the Spirit appears to be to enable the Christian to live a holy life. In the context of Romans 8:9, where Paul describes the indwelling as the mark of the believer, he enjoins his readers to live by the Spirit (Rom. 8:1–12). Just previously Paul had depicted the self-defeating experience of those who live by their own efforts. Even the most well-intentioned attempts at pleasing God backfire into sin. Our bodies do not want to obey our minds (Rom. 7). But the Spirit gives us a new life inside of our mortal bodies so that we can have victory over the vicious circle of fallenness.

Because of the indwelling, the human spirit stands in an immediate relation to the divine Spirit. In two places, Paul points to the Holy Spirit inside of us as the one who says "Abba—Father" to God on our behalf (Gal. 4:6; Rom. 8:16). Our very inner being is now under the direction of the Spirit of God. This fact is stated most dramatically in 2 Peter 1:4,

[11]Michael Green, *I Believe in the Holy Spirit* (Grand Rapids: Eerdmans, 1975), 77.

where Christians are said to "participate in the divine nature." This statement means not that we have somehow monistically become God but that we may now share in God's very nature, undoubtedly because of his indwelling of us.

This truth of the indwelling may be described as mystical. It fulfills our basic requirements to fall under the working definition—namely, it represents an unmediated link to an absolute. In this case the believer is directly joined to God, the Holy Spirit, who indwells him or her. Here there is no necessity of a traditional mystical experience, as described by William James, for example. What we have here is the state of habitual union, as labeled by Kiekhefer.[12] And let us remind ourselves that Kiekhefer maintains that even Meister Eckhart does not mean to say more than that (see the discussion in chapter 6). In any event, such a direct union with God and human being can be at the heart of an ontological mysticism and thus also within the New Testament experience.

In Christ

A number of New Testament scholars have advocated a mystical understanding of the Pauline phrase "in Christ," but none more so than Adolf Deissmann.[13] Deissmann uses a definition of mysticism similar to ours. He says, "Thus I am no innovator, but rather seek to re-establish the old German usage, when I understand '*Mystik*' in the wider sense and give the name *Mystik* to every religious tendency that discovers the way to God direct through inner experience without the mediation of reasoning. The constitutive element in mysti-

---

[12]Kiekhefer, "Meister Eckhart's Conception," 203–25.

[13]Deissmann, *Paul*. See also A. J. Gordon, *In Christ, or, The Believer's Union with His Lord* (Boston: Gould and Lincoln, 1874); James S. Stewart, *A Man in Christ: The Vital Elements of St. Paul's Religion* (New York: Harper and Brothers, n.d.); William A. Mueller, "The Mystical Union," in *Basic Christian Doctrines*, ed. Carl F. H. Henry (Grand Rapids: Baker, 1962), 206–12; F. F. Bruce, "Was Paul a Mystic?" *Reformed Theological Review* 34 (1975): 66–75.

cism is immediacy of contact with the deity."[14] And Deissmann believes that such a phenomenon can be demonstrated in Paul's theology.

One of Deissmann's first lines of support is the observation that "in Christ" or "in the Lord" occurs in Paul's writings 164 times. Deissmann considers this phrase to be the "peculiarly Pauline expression of the most intimate possible fellowship of the Christian with the living spiritual Christ."[15] Paul's Christianity centered on this direct fellowship with Christ, and so Paul found the formula to be the clearest statement of that reality. Consequently the two statements "Christ in me" and "I in Christ" are two sides of the same coin. James S. Stewart endorses the same concept with the observation, "The heart of Paul's religion is union with Christ."[16]

Contemporary Christians have grown up with this Pauline language as standard vocabulary of their faith, thereby possibly removing its original impact. On routine reading, "in Christ" seems to convey nothing more than being in some way related to Christ, for example, as follower to Leader or as sinner to Savior. But as Deissmann and others have observed, if we go back to a fresh reading of this phrase, it becomes apparent that it would be a very peculiar way of expressing simply an external relationship. The significance of "in Christ" is that it exhibits the most intimate communion of the Christian with the resurrected Jesus.

According to Deissmann, Paul is a "reacting mystic."[17] An acting mystic is one who strives to achieve the intimate relationship with God. Deissmann suggests that this characteristic may have been true of Paul prior to his conversion. But when he became a Christian, he realized that communion with God is the result of God's gracious act alone. The believer can only accept God's grace as it is given to him or her.

---

[14]Deissmann, *Paul*, 149.
[15]Ibid., 140.
[16]Stewart, *Man in Christ*, 147.
[17]Deissmann, *Paul*, 149–55.

Paul's description of his being caught up into third heaven in 2 Corinthians is a fruitful source of speculation. As we have seen, some Christian writers have equated this experience with his Damascus road experience, namely, with his conversion.[18] Others have simply made the experience the epitome of the mystic life of Paul.[19] Recently it has been suggested that there may be evidence here of a mystical streak in Paul's Jewish heritage.[20] Along the line of many other Jews of his day, Paul, in his younger days, may well have been in pursuit of the *devekuth* experience. But one thing is clear: In the passage in question, Paul deliberately subordinates the experience to the grace of God in all of the trials of his life and ministry. Thus Deissmann's conclusion that at the time of his conversion Paul left the active quest for mystical experience behind is plausible.

Another category that Deissmann places on Paul is that of being a "*communio* mystic."[21] Again there is a contrast, this time with a *unio* mystic. The question is between oneness with God *(unio)* and fellowship *(communio). Unio* mysticism would be monism, which is not taught in Paul. The believer is transformed and brought into communion with Christ. One is not deified, nor is one's individuality obliterated.

Now Stewart rightly comments that Deissmann tends to push his insights too far. "The question may however be raised—Is the full mystical meaning present in *every* occurrence of the phrase in Paul's epistles? Probably not. This is Deissmann's mistake. Having made his discovery, he is inclined to apply it everywhere without exception. He forces his key into every lock." Nonetheless, Stewart agrees that the majority of "in Christ" passages have the mystical meaning. In fact, he concurs that "in some degree, then, *every real*

---

[18]Harkness, *Mysticism*, 43.

[19]See Underhill, *Mystic Way*, 157–209.

[20]Peter Schafer, "New Testament and Hekhalot Literature: The Journey into Heaven in Paul and in Merkavah Mysticism," *Journal of Jewish Studies* 35 (1984): 19–35.

[21]Deissmann, *Paul*, 152.

Christian is a mystic in the Pauline sense."[22] Let us look at how this commitment affects other crucial issues in Pauline Christianity in Stewart's eyes.

We have already made the point that the mystical communion is the direct work of God's grace, received through the response of faith. Stewart defines the characteristic Pauline understanding of faith as "utter self-abandonment to the God revealed in Jesus Christ."[23] There are many other dimensions to faith, but this is the most crucial one. Becoming "in Christ" means letting Christ take over.

Stewart observes that for Paul to be "in Christ" means not just a positional change, but it carries over into the life of the believer. He stresses the burial and resurrection with Jesus (Rom. 6). In fact, Stewart claims that for Paul "this life into possession of which souls entered by conversion was *nothing else than the life of Christ Himself.* He shares his very being with them."[24]

This observation also clarifies Paul's understanding of ethics for the believer. Although one is admitted into fellowship with Christ by faith alone, apart from the merit of good works, Paul is no antinomian. *Communio* with Christ means that we will share Christ's attitude to sin and his power to overcome sin. Nor does it mean that the Christian no longer has any struggle with sin. Thus the reality of being in Christ also governs the believer's life.[25]

Finally, Stewart points out a major characteristic of Paul's mysticism—the eschatological dimension. Frequently mystical religion is contrasted with historical religion, where the former is considered static and concerned only with present spirituality, while the latter is oriented to time and to future fulfillment. But in Paul the two aspects do not exclude each other. Stewart argues that it is precisely because of Paul's present mystical reality that he is directed to the fulfillment

[22]Stewart, *Man in Christ*, 157, 162.
[23]Ibid., 182.
[24]Ibid., 193.
[25]Ibid., 194-200.

in the future. He says, "There is really nothing incongruous about this: vital Christianity from the days when Jesus preached the Gospel of a Kingdom which was at once a present reality and a future hope, has always held the two positions together."[26] Thus the mystical union encompasses the believer's past, present, and future.

Albert Schweitzer was well known for his appropriation of the idea of Christ-mysticism in Paul. He summarizes: "The fundamental thought of Pauline mysticism runs thus: I am in Christ; in Him I know myself as a being who is raised above this sensuous, sinful, and transient world and already belongs to the transcendent; in Him I am assured of resurrection; in Him I am a child of God." But Schweitzer also emphasizes that some passages that mention being in Christ refer not to the position of an individual believer but to the church collectively.[27]

We mentioned already that Stewart charges Deissmann with reductionism. Other scholars have gone further in pointing out nonmystical meaning in verses where "in Christ" appears. G. E. Ladd mentions juridical and eschatological interpretations.[28] However, we already stated that these categories need not exclude the mystical dimension. In any event, if of the 164 verses only a few carry the mystical meaning expounded above, it would still suffice in bearing important testimony to this mystical side of New Testament thought. For example, Philippians 4:7 states, "And the peace of God, which transcends all understanding, will guard your hearts and your minds in Christ Jesus." Clearly there is no mysticism of the perennial philosophy variety to be found in this verse. The verse indicates, rather, the position of the believer in Christ. Christ is not the object of the believer's

---

[26]Ibid., 202.

[27]Albert Schweitzer, *The Mysticism of Paul the Apostle*, trans. William Montgomery (New York: Macmillan, 1955), 3, 23.

[28]G. E. Ladd, *A Theology of the New Testament* (Grand Rapids: Eerdmans, 1974), 481–82.

faith, but the believer's location. Because one is in Christ, one enjoys God's peace.

A similar point could be made for Romans 8:39, which concludes that nothing "will be able to separate us from the love of God that is in Christ Jesus our Lord." The believer is here provided with confidence in his or her security for one reason only: the reality in Christ Jesus. These verses and many others exemplify the kind of mysticism attributed to Paul by Deissmann and Stewart.

Sons of God

Albert Schweitzer made a very significant point in connection with Pauline mysticism, namely, that "in Paul there is no God-mysticism; only a Christ-mysticism by means of which man comes into relation to God."[29] The mediatorship of Christ is necessary for communion with God. But it brings us adoption as children of God (Rom. 8:14; Gal. 3:26).

We need to be careful not to squeeze too much literal meaning out of a metaphor. But neither ought we to empty the metaphor. The whole point of the expression is that we are now in a relationship to God that is deeper and more intimate than that of slaves, followers, or disciples. Indeed, the author of Hebrews points out that as children of God we share Christ's origin and are his siblings (Heb. 2:10–11).

This thought can be continued by reference to unity passages in John 17:20–21.[30] Jesus prays for unity among all believers along the model of the unity of Father and Son and then asks that the believers may become one in the divine unity. Certainly this passage should not be understood monistically. The Eastern concept of *theosis* is also too strong and concept-laden to impose on this New Testament saying. But there can be no doubt that here we have one of the strongest statements of the intimacy of our relationship with God.

---

[29]Schweitzer, *Mysticism of Paul*, 3.

[30]See M. P. John, "Johannine Mysticism," *Indian Journal of Theology* 5 (1956): 15–21.

However we may want to interpret Meister Eckhart, it is definitely this unity with God that he emphasized. And yet we can make a strong case that Eckhart was doing no more than expounding what we read in John 17. He expostulates, "Thus perfectly to have given up one's own is to be merged with God, and then anyone who will touch the man must first touch God, for he is wholly within God and God is around him, as my cap is around my head, and to touch me one must first touch my clothing."[31] Is Eckhart saying more here, or less, than Jesus when he prays for us "that all of them may be one, Father, just as you are in me and I am in you. May they also be in us so that the world may believe that you have sent me" (John 17:21)? Two observations give direction to this point of unity. First, corporate unity of the believers is a part of the plan. Second, Jesus gives the unity a purpose, namely, to bring the world to believe in him (which underscores the point that we are not just dealing with an eschatological ideal). Thus we have communion with God, the Father, through Christ, the Son.

Three lines of mystical import thus exist in the New Testament: the indwelling of the Spirit, the communion "in Christ," and the intimate relationship with the Father. And once we mention these three points side by side, an important conclusion emerges. Although Jesus Christ stands at the center of every aspect of the believer's life, it would be wrong to claim that the New Testament knows only of a "Christ-mysticism." The intimate personal relationship with God extends to Father and Holy Spirit as well. Thus in the final analysis what we find in the New Testament is Trinitarian mysticism. And here we do make contact again with Eastern Orthodoxy, where the spiritual life is seen as "a participation in the divine life of the Holy Trinity."[32]

---

[31]Meister Eckhart, "The Talks of Instruction," in *Meister Eckhart*, trans. Raymond B. Blakney (New York: Harper and Row, 1941), 16.

[32]Lossky, *Mystical Theology*, 48.

The Nature of New Testament Mysticism

In sum, then, a picture emerges from the New Testament of a unique kind of mysticism: the Christian's intimate link to the triune God. The entire focus is on a reality that is predicated of each person who believes in Jesus Christ. It neither entails nor is entailed by a unique experience. Also there is no direct revelatory import.

We need to ask why we want to call these realities mystical. This question can be construed in different ways, so it must be addressed on several levels.

At one level it could be suggested that the term "mysticism" is inappropriate because what is reported in the New Testament falls short in important ways of "true" mysticism. For example, it meets neither Stace's seven points nor James's four points of description (see chapter 2 above). Thus it might be best to report the realities without applying the label "mysticism." This argument probably has motivated much of the rejection of Deissmann's categorization. The truths are maintained, but they are not considered mystical.

In reply, we can refer to our earlier argumentation that there is no standard mysticism. Even though there may be some general patterns and working definitions, there is no obligatory set of laws for deciding what is or is not mysticism. Each form of mysticism is unique. Thus on the basis of the objection there could be no mysticism at all, since each tradition would fall short of the ideal. In the final analysis whether the New Testament realities are mystical cannot be decided on the basis of objective standards.

At a second level, the word "mystical" may be too misleading to use in this context. It may have taken on a particular meaning by and large (perhaps the Stacian monistic understanding), and to use it in the New Testament context may only muddy the waters. Even if the word might be used legitimately, it would probably detract from clear communication. Although the present account is probably immune from most of the critiques that Arthur L. Johnson brought against mysticism, he might still want to say that by using the term "mysticism," we are associating ourselves with the problems he has uncovered.

This is a powerful argument against our use of the term "mysticism" here, and the only way it can be answered is by showing that there are indeed compelling reasons for its use. In any event, if the discussion comes down entirely to arbitrary use of a dispensable word, nothing is to be gained by insisting on maintaining it. But words do express certain meanings, and if a particular meaning is best expressed by a certain word, then that word ought to be used.

As we have seen, mysticism does not come with a ready-made standard definition. We chose a very general definition for this study (i.e. an unmediated link to an absolute) because we felt that this definition, rather than a preoccupation with experience, comes closest to the heart of mysticism. Now, this definition does describe mysticism. It may need to be revised, but it is neither arbitrary nor dispensable. And of course it fits the New Testament realities perfectly. The word "mysticism" is appropriate here because what is given here is one form of mysticism. If our general definition of mysticism is defensible and if we have interpreted the New Testament accurately, then the New Testament realities are truly a form of mysticism.

At a third level, while we may grant that it may be accurate and legitimate to use the term "mysticism," what is to be gained by it? Everything that is said ought to be true, but not everything that is true ought to be said. What possible positive advantage can be gained by using a controversial term with some awkward connotations?

We can reply to this version of the objection in a number of ways. Not all the "awkward connotations" are undesirable. If "mystical" carries the connotations of the supernatural, of that which cannot be understood with human reason, and of a direct relationship with the divine, then that is exactly what needs to be conveyed. Let us examine this concern in more detail.

In the course of his many legitimate criticisms of mysticism, Arthur L. Johnson depicts a thoroughly rational understanding of the Christian life. "Knowledge of spiritual matters is always linked to God's propositional revelation, the written Word. . . . If this means that there is always danger of error in our process of coming to knowledge of God, then so be it!" And again, "We do not relate to persons through subjective urges. . . . Why then should we see our relationship to the Holy Spirit in emotional, or psychological terms, rather than in conceptual ones?"[33] Thus, if I understand Johnson correctly, the entire Christian experience must be filtered through the Christian's mind. It appears that the Christian life could then be reduced to this pattern: the Christian reads a Bible passage, recognizes a specific truth, and takes pains to put it into practice. The Holy Spirit apparently comes into play as facilitator only. As the human does what he or she is supposed to do, the Holy Spirit helps that one by providing the ability to do it, but it is the Christian who actually does the work by following the two steps of understanding the obligations and carrying them out.

But something important is missing from this description, namely, the fundamental reality that we described above. In addition to emotional, psychological, and conceptual ways of interacting, there can be a basic ontological relationship. The Holy Spirit is present and acting in the Christian's life. He is the enabler, but he is more than that; he is also frequently the doer. In Murray's words, "by way of eminence, however, the agent [of our sanctification] is the Holy Spirit."[34] This is not the place to develop an entire theology of sanctification. The point is that the New Testament understanding of the Christian life does not make much sense apart from the direct supernatural work of God any more than its understanding of our salvation does (see Gal. 3:3).

But as soon as we have reached this conclusion, the

---

[33]Johnson, "Mysticism and Evangelical Thought," 25.

[34]John Murray, "Sanctification (The Law)," in *Basic Christian Doctrine*, ed. Carl F. H. Henry (Grand Rapids: Baker, 1962), 227–33.

mystical becomes an important category. We do not have to follow Watchman Nee and rewrite the New Testament by bringing it into line with Eastern mystical thought; there is something uniquely mystical in the New Testament already, namely, God's direct work within us.

Every age or every tradition in the history of the church seems to fall prey to overemphasizing one particular avenue of God's work in our lives. Medieval Christianity centered on sacramental mysticism. In response, Protestantism has emphasized the role of the Word of God in the life of his people. God uses study and preaching as his instrument. But it would also be a mistake to fall into the error of rationalism, namely, that God works only through our rational response to verbal messages. Philippians 2:13 reminds us that "it is God who works in you to will and to act according to his good purpose."

This reality stands at the end of the quest constituted by this inquiry. The Christian knows for a fact something that others can only strive for in vain—he or she is directly, supernaturally related to God, the Creator and Sustainer of the universe. And this relationship is so close that it can be described only with the most intimate expressions: "indwelled," "in Christ," "adopted as sons," and, even more audaciously, "participating in the divine nature." These truths go far beyond the cognitive and rational; they are given facts. Consequently the Christian's life is lived optimally on the plane of these facts. To ignore them is tantamount to pushing a car through sheer muscle power rather than relying on the engine. Any wholesale dismissal of everything "mystical" in favor of the purely cognitive would direct us away from these supernatural facts.

Let us clarify a little further how rationality functions in this context. There is a long-standing tradition of confusion between something being logical and its being deducible. The term "rational" can apply to either. By the former we mean that some reality or a proposition expressing it conforms to the basic laws of logic—(identity, contradiction, excluded middle). By the latter term we can mean that some truth is known on the basis of rational deduction (e.g. a geometric theorem). Now it is clear that a truth may fit the first category and be perfectly logical, without it fitting into the second category, that of being known directly on the basis of reason. Much of the supposed illogicality in theology is not that at all, but merely the limit of our epistemologies.

Something similar must be true with regard to New Testament mysticism. It is not irrational in the sense that the categories of logic are exceeded, suspended, or transcended. Nevertheless, it would be a mistake to think that therefore the realities described are entirely comprehended by human reason. The relationship of a finite creature to the infinite God must always be larger than our understanding. (And thus we have the need for analogical representation argued for above.) If then the term "mysticism" bears the connotation of incomprehensibility, it is not inappropriate. And at the same time, the fact of direct supernatural action cannot be overemphasized.

Conclusion and Agenda

Let us recapitulate the argument of this book as it developed. After a general description of mysticism, I defined it very generally as an unmediated link to an absolute. I stressed that the story of any particular mysticism is indispensable for understanding it; exclusive preoccupation with the experiential side of mysticism can sidetrack the analysis considerably.

I took a mediating position in the controversy of whether mysticism is a perennial philosophy. The attempt to identify a universal core of mysticism suffers from an acute case of reductionism. Yet to say that all mystical traditions are so unique that they have nothing in common does not hold either. There must be some general truths about the unmediated link to the absolute, perhaps by family resemblance.

That conclusion naturally weakened the argument from unanimity, the attempt to show that there is objective reality behind mystical experience because all true mystics say similar things. Since they do not, that argument does not work. I argued that human beings seem to have a general faculty for mystical experience that can be activated by many different causes—objective and otherwise. Consequently, the story of a tradition becomes paramount, and the truth claims made by mystics need to be adjudicated on general objective grounds. In other words, if there is truth in Hindu, Jewish, or Christian mysticism, that can only be so because Hinduism, Judaism, or Christianity are true, not because one or the other has the best form of mysticism.

I addressed the problem of the supposed phenomenon of ineffability in mysticism. After evaluating different explanations, I concluded, first, that the language of the mystic cannot be totally ineffable, and, second, that the conceptual and linguistic difficulties are satisfactorily explained in the same way as problems with religious language in general, perhaps with a system of analogy.

The first look at mysticism in Christendom was taken for didactic purposes, essentially to learn the lesson of errors to be avoided. Our goal was to find out if there was room for mysticism in uncompromised biblical Christianity. The conclusions of this inquiry were presented above in this chapter. There is mystical reality in the believer's relationship to the divine Trinity through adoption as God's child, a position "in Christ," and the indwelling of the Holy Spirit.

But this chapter ends with a paradox. We have claimed that mysticism is a very important aspect of New Testament theology. And yet there is no mystical experience to be sought. There is no truth to be learned through New Testament mysticism. There is no plan of asceticism or meditation to actualize this mystical reality. Rather, there are two important imperatives. The first is, "Believe in the Lord Jesus!" (Acts 16:31). Immediately the realities discussed above are actualized. The second is, "Live . . . . according to the Spirit!" (Rom. 8:5) The point now is to live a life in the light of the fact that those realities are given by God's grace. Christians do not need to seek present realities, but to enjoy them. As they yield to the work of God, the Holy Spirit produces a new supernatural life in them.

This book is not the place to give a full description of the Christian life with all of its injunctions, blessings, and anticipations. The note on which we may conclude here is that none of it would make any sense apart from Christians' mystical communion with God in Christ, their Lord and Savior.

Bibliography

Alston, William P. "Ineffability." *Philosophical Review* 65 (1956): 506–22.

Appleby, Peter C. "Mysticism and Ineffability." *International Journal for Philosophy of Religion* 11 (1980): 143–65.

Augustine. *The Confessions of St. Augustine*. Trans. John K. Ryan. Garden City, N.Y.: Doubleday Anchor, 1960.

Barrois, George A. "Mysticism—What Is It?" *Theology Today* 4 (1947): 190–202.

Bergson, Henri. *The Two Sources of Morality and Religion*. Garden City, N.Y.: Doubleday Anchor, 1935.

Broad, C. D. *Religion, Philosophy, and Psychical Research*. London: Routledge and Kegan Paul, 1953.

Bruce, F. F. "Was Paul a Mystic?" *Reformed Theological Review* 34 (1975): 66–75.

Butler, Cuthbert. *Western Mysticism: The Teaching of SS Augustine, Gregory, and Bernard on Contemplation and the Contemplative Life*. New York: Dutton, 1924.

Corduan, Winfried. *Handmaid to Theology: An Essay in Philosophical Prolegomena*. Grand Rapids: Baker, 1981.

_____. "Humility and Commitment: An Approach to Modern Hermeneutics." *Themelios* 11 (1986): 83–88.

_____. "Philosophical Presuppositions Affecting Hermeneutics." In *Hermeneutics, Inerrancy, and the Bible*, ed. Earl D. Radmacher and Robert D. Preus. Grand Rapids: Zondervan, 1984.

de Bary, William Theodore. *Sources of Indian Tradition*. 2 vols. New York: Columbia University Press, 1958.

Deikman, Arthur J. *The Observing Self: Mysticism and Psychotherapy.* Boston: Beacon Press, 1982.

Deissmann, Adolf. *Paul: A Study in Social and Religious History.* New York: Harper and Row, 1957.

Easley, Kendell H. *"To Pneuma tou Theou Oikei en Humin: A Literal Indwelling by the Spirit-as-Substance or a Figurative Reference to a Personal Relationship?"* Paper presented to the Evangelical Theological Society, November 1987.

Eckhart, Johannes (Meister). *Parisian Questions and Prologues.* Trans. Armand A. Maurer. Toronto: Pontifical Institute of Medieval Studies, 1974.

————. "The Talks of Instruction." In *Meister Eckhart,* trans. Raymond B. Blakney. New York: Harper and Row, 1941.

Findlay, John. "The Logic of Mysticism." *Religious Studies* 2 (1966): 145–62.

Garside, Bruce. "Language and the Interpretation of Mystical Experience." In *International Journal for Philosophy of Religion* 3 (1972): 93–102.

Geisler, Norman L., and Corduan, Winfried. *Philosophy of Religion.* 2nd ed. Grand Rapids: Baker, 1988.

Gordon, A. J. *In Christ; or, The Believer's Union with His Lord.* Boston: Gould and Lincoln, 1874.

Green, Deirdre. "Unity in Diversity." *Scottish Journal of Religious Studies* 3 (1982): 46–58.

Green, Michael. *I Believe in the Holy Spirit.* Grand Rapids: Eerdmans, 1975.

Happold, F. C. *Mysticism: A Study and an Anthology.* Baltimore: Penguin Books, 1963.

Harkness, Georgia. *Mysticism: Its Meaning and Message.* Nashville: Abingdon, 1973.

Hatab, Lawrence J. "Mysticism and Language." *International Philosophical Quarterly* 22 (1982): 51–64.

Hattiangadi, J. N. "Why Is Indian Religion Mystical?" *Journal of Indian Philosophy* 3 (1975): 253–58.

Hoffman, Robert. "Logic, Meaning, and Mystical Intuition." *Philosophical Studies* 11 (1960): 65–70.

Huxley, Aldous. *The Doors of Perception.* New York: Harper and Row, 1954.

————. *The Perennial Philosophy.* Cleveland: World, 1962.

Inge, William Ralph. *Christian Mysticism.* New York: Scribner's, 1933.

James, William. *The Varieties of Religious Experience.* New York: Collier, 1961.

John, M. P. "Johannine Mysticism" *Indian Journal of Theology* 5 (1956): 15–21.

Johnson, Arthur L. *Faith Misguided: Exposing the Dangers of Mysticism.* Chicago: Moody Press, 1988.

————. "Mysticism and Evangelical Thought." *Bulletin of the Evangelical Philosophical Society* 8 (1985): 18–27. (This article is listed incorrectly under the name of James D. Spiceland.)

Jones, Richard H. "Experience and Conceptualization in Mystical Knowledge." *Zygon* 18 (1983): 139–65.

Jones, Rufus M. *Some Exponents of Mystical Religion.* Nashville: Abingdon, 1930.

Katz, Steven T., ed. *Mysticism and Philosophical Analysis.* New York: Oxford University Press, 1978.

Kellenberger, J. "The Ineffabilities of Mysticism." *American Philosophical Quarterly* 16 (1979): 307–15.

Keller, Carl A. "Mystical Literature." In *Mysticism and Philosophical Analysis,* ed. Steven T. Katz. New York: Oxford University Press, 1978.

Kiekhefer, Richard. "Meister Eckhart's Conception of Union with God." *Harvard Theological Review* 71 (1978): 203–25.

Kohl, Marvin. "The Unanimity Argument and the Mystics." *Hibbert Journal* 58 (1959): 268–75.

Krishan, Daya. "Mysticism and the Problem of Intelligibility." *Journal of Religion* 34 (1954): 101–5.

Kristo, Jure. "The Interpretation of Religious Experience: What Do Mystics Intend When They Talk about Their Experiences?" *Journal of Religion* 62 (1982): 21–38.

Ladd, G. E. *A Theology of the New Testament.* Grand Rapids: Eerdmans, 1974.

Lossky, Vladimir. *The Mystical Theology of the Eastern Church.* Cambridge: Clark, 1944.

MacIntyre, Alasdair. "Is Religious Language So Idiosyncratic That We Can Hope for No Account of It?" In *Religious Language and the Problem of Religious Knowledge,* ed. Ronald E. Santoni. Bloomington: Indiana University Press, 1968.

Martin, D. D. "Mysticism." In *Evangelical Dictionary of Theology,* ed. Walter Elwell. Grand Rapids: Baker, 1984.

Matilal, B. "Mysticism and Reality: Ineffability." In *Journal of Indian Philosophy* 3 (1975): 217–52.

Maurer, Armand A. *Medieval Philosophy.* New York: Random House, 1962.

Melchert, Norman. "Mystical Experience and Ontological Claims." *Philosophy and Phenomenological Research* 37 (1977): 445–63.

Mueller, William A. "The Mystical Union." In *Basic Christian Doctrines,* ed. Carl F. H. Henry. Grand Rapids: Baker, 1962.

Murray, John. "Sanctification (The Law)." In *Basic Christian Doctrines,* ed. Carl F. H. Henry. Grand Rapids: Baker, 1962.

Nee, Watchman. *The Spiritual Man.* New York: Christian Fellowship, 1968.

Neihardt, John G. *Black Elk Speaks: Being the Life Story of a Holy Man of the Oglala Sioux.* New York: Pocket Books, 1932.

Nevins, Stanley A. "Mystical Consciousness and the Problem of Personal Identity." *Philosophy Today* 20 (1976): 149–56.

Oakes, Robert. "Religious Experience and Epistemological Miracles: A Moderate Defense of Theistic Mysticism." *International Journal for Philosophy of Religion* 12 (1981): 97–110.

Otto, Rudolf. *Mysticism East and West.* New York: Collier, 1960.

Perovich, Anthony N., Jr. "Mysticism and the Philosophy of Science." *Journal of Religion* 65 (1985): 63–82.

Plantinga, Alvin. *God and Other Minds.* Ithaca, N.Y.: Cornell University Press, 1967.

Pletcher, Gary K. "Mysticism, Contradiction, and Ineffability." *American Philosophical Quarterly* 10 (1973): 201–11.

Schäfer, Peter. "New Testament and Hekhalot Literature: The Journey into Heaven in Paul and in Merkavah Mysticism." *Journal of Jewish Studies* 35 (1984): 18–35.

Schleiermacher, Friedrich. *Hermeneutics: The Handwritten Manuscripts.* Ed. Heinz Kimmerle, trans. James Duke and Jack Forstman. Missoula, Mont.: Scholars Press, 1977.

Scholem, Gershom G. *Major Trends in Jewish Mysticism.* New York: Schocken, 1941.

Schweitzer, Albert. *The Mysticism of Paul the Apostle.* Trans. William Montgomery. New York: Macmillan, 1955.

Smart, Ninian. "Interpretation and Mystical Experience." *Religious Studies* 1 (1965): 75–88.

————. "Understanding Religious Experience." In *Mysticism and Philosophical Analysis*, ed. Steven T. Katz. New York: Oxford University Press, 1978.

Stace, W. T. *Mysticism and Philosophy.* New York: St. Martin's Press, Jeremy P. Tarcher, 1960.

Stewart, James S. *A Man in Christ: The Vital Elements of St. Paul's Religion.* New York: Harper and Brothers, n.d.

Thomas Aquinas. *Summa Theologica.*

Tozer, A. W. *Man: The Dwelling Place of God.* Harrisburg, Pa.: Christian Publications, 1966.

Underhill, Evelyn. *Mysticism: A Study in the Nature and Development of Man's Spiritual Consciousness.* New York: Dutton, 1911.

————. *The Mystic Way: A Psychological Study in Christian Origins.* New York: Dutton, 1913.

Wainwright, William J. "Stace and Mysticism." *Journal of Religion* 50 (1970): 139–54.

Watts, Alan. *The Supreme Identity: An Essay in Oriental Metaphysic and the Christian Religion.* New York: Random House, 1972.

Whitehead, Alfred North. *Religion in the Making.* New York: World, 1960.

Wittgenstein, Ludwig. *Philosophical Investigations.* 3rd ed. Trans. G. E. M. Anscombe. New York: Macmillan, 1958.

Zaehner, R. C. *Mysticism: Sacred and Profane.* London: Oxford University Press, 1957.

Index